The
Virtual Body
of Christ

in a Suffering World

The Virtual
Body of Christ

in a Suffering World

Deanna A. Thompson

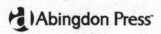
Nashville

THE VIRTUAL BODY OF CHRIST IN A SUFFERING WORLD

Library of Congress Cataloging-in-Publication Data

Names: Thompson, Deanna A., 1966- author.
Title: The virtual Body of Christ in a suffering world / Deanna A. Thompson.
Description: Nashville, TN : Abingdon Press, 2016. | Includes bibliographical
   references.
Identifiers: LCCN 2016021750| ISBN 9781501815188 (pbk.) | ISBN 9781501815195
   (ebook)
Subjects: LCSH: Internet--Religious aspects--Christianity. | Internet in
   church work. | Online social networks—Religious aspects—Christianity.
Classification: LCC BR99.74 .T56 2016 | DDC 261.5/2—dc23 LC record
available at https://lccn.loc.gov/2016021750

16 17 18 19 20 21 22 23 24 25—10 9 8 7 6 5 4 3 2 1
MANUFACTURED IN THE UNITED STATES OF AMERICA

For my brother, Noel Thompson

SMS

Contents

Contents

SMS

Acknowledgments

In my experience, a writing project is never a solitary endeavor. And just as is the case in all aspects of my life, I am indebted to so many who have helped this project become a reality. First and foremost, my most profound gratitude goes to all of those who have surrounded me and my family since my diagnosis with stage IV cancer in 2008 with love, care, and concern in the actual and virtual worlds. You all have opened up for me a hope not just for my own future but also for the potential within this new world of digitization to better care for and support one another in the most awful times of our lives. Thank you for one of the biggest surprises of my life.

Within the vast virtual body of Christ, there are a number of people who deserve mention for their distinctive roles in helping this project come to fruition:

To the CaringBridge organization and founder Sona Mehring, who through their more than half a million websites have provided a most powerful tool that can help care for and support those in crisis.

To Krista Tippett, who first identified the virtual body of Christ as an important theological insight for our day in her foreword to my theo-memoir *Hoping for More: Having Cancer, Talking Faith, and Accepting Grace.*

To David Lose, who, after hearing my first public presentation on the virtual body of Christ at a Reimagining Faith Formation conference at Luther Seminary in summer 2014, told me, "You have to publish this *right away.*"

To Bishop Elaine Sauer of the Evangelical Lutheran Church of Canada and the gathering of First Call pastors I met with in fall 2014 to dig deeply into and debate the possibilities and pitfalls of embracing the virtual body of Christ.

To David Teel, wise and ever-encouraging editor of this project and friend from Vanderbilt Graduate School days, for his shepherding the vision through the process of book making.

To Hamline faculty secretary Wendy Werdin, for her editorial assistance.

Acknowledgments

To my father, Rev. Mervin Thompson, for arranging for me to share this vision of the virtual body of Christ at the 2015 Hope Leadership Conference at Hope Lutheran in West Des Moines, Iowa, and to both him and my mother, Jackie Thompson, for their constant support and enthusiasm for and insightful feedback on drafts of the project.

To my daughters' continued love and support. Specifically to Linnea Peterson, who edited an entire draft of the manuscript, and whose fabulous editorial suggestions and incisive perspectives on our digitized lives from the vantage point of a young adult have been invaluable to this project, and to Annika Peterson, for her unflagging support and enthusiasm for this project and gentle attempts to keep me semicurrent regarding emerging developments in virtual communication.

To my husband, Neal Peterson, for walking every step of this journey with me, for his abiding faith, love, and care, and for his acceptance of the healing gifts of the virtual body of Christ that continue to come our way.

And finally, to my brother, Noel Thompson, for creating the CaringBridge website for us in those grief-filled days of December 2008 and opening up the possibility for us to be carried and converted by all those who made up the virtual body of Christ when we did not think we could go on. To him this book is dedicated.

Part One
The Virtual World Is Our World

Introduction

Embraced by the Virtual Body of Christ

A Conversion Story

Not many years ago, I had a dim view of the Internet's ability to create networks of trust and support. Living and working with others constantly connected to—and distracted by—their digital tools left me skeptical that any new relational depth was being plumbed through our increasingly digitized lives. I did not own a cell phone and was quick to judge others whose attention focused more on their hand-held devices than on the people sitting next to them.

Then I got sick. Really sick.

In a matter of months, I went from being a healthy forty-one-year-old religion professor, wife, and mother to a virtual invalid with a broken back, a stage IV cancer diagnosis, and a grim prognosis for the future.

To keep family and friends updated during the early days following the diagnosis, my brother proposed the creation of a CaringBridge site, an online social network that connects people who have serious issues with those who care about them. Because I was a digital skeptic, I imagine that if I hadn't been on so much oxycodone I would have protested setting up such a site.

Once the site went live, news of my diagnosis spread quickly; just as quickly, loved ones, friends, and even strangers signed up to receive my CaringBridge updates. From my posts about what stage IV cancer was doing to my body to entries on the grief of having to resign from my very full and wonderful life, my cries were met not just with responses on the CaringBridge site but also with e-mails, cards, packages, visits, and calls from people from all corners of my life. It was shocking to realize that through virtual connectedness via a website, I

3

was surrounded by a cloud of witnesses greater than any I could have previously imagined.

Even after growing up in the church and acquiring a doctorate in theology, I had never given the church universal much thought in life before cancer. I have always been a big fan of the local church, extolling the virtues of participation in local communities of faith that at their best offer glimpses of the heavenly city where there's no more crying, no more dying, only light, only love. I have long believed that when the church is being the church, it is present in profound and compassionate ways with those who suffer. As the daughter of a pastor, I have witnessed local churches time and again embody the hands and feet of Christ in their ministries to those in pain. In life precancer, any talk of the church universal always seemed abstract to me, largely removed from the daily realities of pain and suffering that fill our lives.

While members of my local church community have most certainly been the hands and feet of Christ in their ministry to me and many others in pain, I have nevertheless been awakened to a new—indeed, almost mystical—understanding of the church universal and the healing effects it has had on my life and the lives of my family and close friends. The church universal is no longer a concept I simply gloss over in the recitation of a creed during worship. I have been surprised and humbled by the ways in which the church universal has become a tangible agent of grace in my life—most shocking for me is experiencing the wideness of the church through virtual reality: that is, the body of Christ incarnated in, with, and through the power of Internet sites like CaringBridge.

This is not to say that before the Internet people were without the benefit of vast networks of prayer and support. But Internet connectivity has exponentially increased the speed and scope of such connections. This experience of the virtual body of Christ has also gifted me with fresh appreciation of the necessarily ecumenical character of the church catholic. Prompted by my entries on Caring-Bridge, many of my friends from the Roman Catholic tradition—the church that holds most tightly to this notion of universality—have embodied Christ to me in powerful and poignant ways. As news of my diagnosis spread, Mass was dedicated to me in India, Sri Lanka, California, as well as closer to home in Minnesota. I have received hundreds of cards from a Catholic parish half a country away where Sunday school classes pray for me weekly. I have been given a medallion blessed and sent on to me by a friend who also happens to be a priest. These traditions of dedicating, blessing, honoring—traditions that make rare appearances in my own Protestant (Lutheran) expressions of church—have made their mark on my soul. To hold the *With God, all things are possible* medallion blessed by my friend brings deep comfort and facilitates a sense of hope for what lies ahead.

Those who have experienced diagnosis of a serious illness or other traumatic event know that what often accompanies experiences of trauma is an inability—especially early on—to put into words what it's like to live in the midst of such trauma. The psalmist captures this when he writes, "I'm so upset I can't even speak" (Ps 77:4b). Those words resonate at a deep level with my experience of being undone by an advanced stage cancer diagnosis in my early forties. Words went away. I initially was at a loss of how to describe my condition (metastatic breast cancer fractured two of my vertebrae and was eating away at my hip, my pelvis—*come again??*) or over what words were available to try and make sense of what was happening to my body, my spirit, my soul.

What is it, then, that those of us who experience this kind of trauma need from those around us (and by implication, from the body of Christ)? Trauma theorist Cathy Caruth describes the challenging negotiation those who work with persons who've been traumatized are faced with: "[It's about] how to help relieve suffering, and how to understand the nature of the suffering, without eliminating the force and truth of the reality that trauma survivors face and quite often try to transmit to us."[1] Relief of suffering, then, is closely linked to those who suffer being able to express the contours of their suffering as well as those who love and care for them understanding those same contours.

My own experience of publically narrating this journey with stage IV cancer virtually on CaringBridge has become a powerful avenue for helping others (and myself) gain deeper knowledge of the particularities of my cancer condition. Spelling out what had happened to me to get to the diagnosis of metastatic breast cancer allowed me to orient myself and everyone else to my unusual and new reality: the breast cancer was not detected through annual mammograms; it metastasized to my bones, fracturing first one then another vertebra in my back. It was diagnosed through a biopsy on my spine. Treatment included radiation to the bones where the cancer was most active: the spine, the pelvis, and the hips. For all of us familiar with the breast cancer drill (finding a lump, biopsying the breast, undergoing a mastectomy, radiating the breast, enduring chemotherapy), my story simply did not map the dominant breast cancer story. Neither did statistics of survival: at the time of my diagnosis in December 2008, studies reported that 80 percent of patients with metastatic breast cancer were dead within five years. My broken back, coupled with the severity of the diagnosis, altered every part of my world. And the ability to have access to a virtual space where I could begin to share the particularities of my story proved a vital tool to help me create a narrative of the suffering and upheaval metastatic breast cancer forced into my life.

But for many who endure traumatic events such as a life-altering diagnosis, it is unnerving to think about publically narrating an illness for hundreds to read and comment on. I agree: it *is* a risky endeavor. Philosopher Annette Baier's insight into possible risks of being vulnerable is applicable to the public sharing of journeys with cancer and other awfulness: "Where one depends on another's good will, one is necessarily vulnerable to the limits of that good will. One leaves others an opportunity to harm one when one trusts, and also shows one's confidence that they will not take it."[2] What Baier helps makes clear is that *any* and *all* attempts at becoming vulnerable by sharing what dealing with such awfulness looks like from the inside carry risk, not just the sharing of vulnerabilities via digital communication but also the sharing done face-to-face. Doing so in cyberspace, however, multiplies the interactions and potentially amplifies the vulnerability.

In the seven years I have been participating in online conversations about life with incurable cancer, there certainly have been responses I have found less than helpful. A couple could even be considered harmful. None of which is qualitatively different than what I've experienced in face-to-face communication. The much more common experience of digital communication about my cancer has been that others' online words of support have nurtured a powerful, healing culture that has been building since my diagnosis. I have found that sharing with hundreds of readers aspects of my grief, my struggles (physical, spiritual, psychological), my setbacks, and my progress better equips those who want to support and care for me and my family to offer more tangible and beneficial care to us all.

One of the most poignant examples of how my own virtual communication of vulnerability has encouraged vulnerability and compassionate care from others in return involves a colleague of mine at the university where I teach. In the decade she and I had worked together prior to the diagnosis, we had never had a substantive discussion about anything personal. A couple months after I got sick, I received an e-mail from this colleague in which she told me about her growing up in Israel as an agnostic Jew and how she often felt on the outside of religious practices like prayer. Reading my postings about my own struggles to pray following the diagnosis, she told me that she became inspired to start praying. Not long after she began praying, she led a group of students to study abroad in Israel. She told me about the group's day at the Western Wall in Jerusalem, where she and another Jewish colleague of mine placed prayers for me into the cracks in the wall. She wrote about how moved she was to see several of our students add their prayers for me to the wall as well. She then recounted for me that in every church the group visited, she would get down on her knees and pray to Jesus for a favor: to heal her friend with cancer. Her message to me ended with this: "I hope I didn't offend Jesus—after all, I'm a Jew and I don't even pray regularly—and there I was, asking Jesus for a favor. I think he'll be ok with that, won't he?"

Words cannot adequately describe what these acts of care and compassion by my colleague have meant to me. That an agnostic Jew would get on her knees in churches throughout Israel to pray for her Christian colleague living with cancer leads me to believe that the Internet is capable of connections that facilitate trust, comfort, even healing in boundary-crossing ways. It seems highly unlikely that without the virtual network my colleague and I both participate in that either of us would have been able to risk the vulnerability with one another that led to the gift of prayer for me in Jerusalem.

What is also clear from this story is that our ever-expanding virtual networks are also going to push us to rethink the boundaries of the church local and universal. For of course it makes no sense to simply declare that my Jewish colleague is now part of the Christian church because she prayed to Jesus on my behalf. As theologian John Thatamanil notes, "When we speak about God, we are heard and overheard by a great cloud of witnesses, a cloud that includes persons of faith who are not part of the Christian community." Going even further, Thatamanil suggests that when Christians reflect on ways in which religious ideas, practices, and commitments intersect between Christians and those outside Christianity, we risk "bearing false witness" against our neighbors if we simply drop them into our already-determined Christian frameworks. "Insofar as our affirmations either implicitly or explicitly challenge or even negate the conviction of others, we run the risk of misunderstanding and mischaracterizing them,"[3] Thatamanil writes. In order to avoid mischaracterization of my dear colleague, it is important to emphasize that the powerful gift of prayer she offered up on my behalf came first of all out of her own Jewish tradition, carried out at a very holy site for Jews in Jerusalem. What happened next was that my colleague took an additional step, physically and theologically crossing into a tradition not her own (a tradition with a fraught relationship to her own, in fact) to address the one Christians like myself believe to be the incarnation of God into the flesh and blood of this world. And this crossing, done in the name of compassion and hope for the healing of a friend, seems to be bound up somehow, someway, to God's universal community of saints. How exactly is still somewhat of a mystery. What I do know is that, for me, my colleague's risky crossing links her hands and feet with the hands and feet of Christ, the first-century Jew whose presence lives on in and through the church universal today.

Since my diagnosis, I have been prayed for by Christian communities across the world, received a sage blessing from a Native American colleague, been prayed for in the synagogues and Hindu temples of friends and colleagues, had Buddhist meditation sessions dedicated to me, and Jesus has even been asked a favor by a Jewish friend who took a gamble on my behalf. When we willingly enter into space filled with another's story of trauma and respond with words and actions that facilitate hope for the one living the trauma, it is a gift, one that crosses and disrupts tidy theological frameworks and previously conceived notions of where the boundaries of the body of Christ lie. Even though it's messy, I do think it is possible to claim that these gifts have arisen from a virtual network, a network that continues to mediate Christ's hands and feet in some kind of tandem with the hands and feet of practitioners of other traditions. All of these gifts enable me to keep walking through the valley of the shadow of cancer, even when the shadow being cast is frightfully long.

Through my experiences of the last seven years of living with cancer, I have come to believe that it is possible to intentionally incarnate the body of Christ virtually in a way that permits and holds my own vulnerability as well as the vulnerabilities of those caring for me. While it is the case that we all can generate instances where the Internet enables people to behave more poorly online than they do in person, it is also the case that examples exist of how at times cyberspace allows us, as journalist Margaret Wertheim suggests, "to do better with the [Internet] than we have done with the physical world."[4] For most of us struggling to live amid the suffering that so often fills our lives, capturing with words the upheaval we face is a continual struggle, and daring to share those words with others takes courage. It is almost always the case that it is less difficult for me to explain how I'm doing in an online post than in a face-to-face conversation. In virtual reality, tears do not make my explanations of my condition unintelligible. When I draft a post about how I'm doing, I can go back and edit out something that sounds more bitter or more optimistic than I intend it to be. In cyberspace, my vulnerabilities often can be better managed than they can be in face-to-face interactions.

This is not to downplay the necessity of others being physically present to us in the worst of times. When awful things happen to us, we need others to be close by, holding a hand, sharing a meal, listening to our attempts to make sense of all that threatens our sense of a meaningful life. But being able to explain how I am doing via digital communications has allowed those close by as well as those far away to have more information as they discern how they might offer support for me and my family. In addition, my posts often allow face-to-face conversations to start from a more informed, advanced place where I often do not have to rehearse the most difficult aspects of the story. The presence of those who care for us—both virtually and in person—is often enhanced by the virtual communication that also is increasingly part of our relationship. All of it together helps the awfulness of what I have gone through seem a little more survivable.

I write this book about the virtual body of Christ because my experience of being supported by a virtual network since my diagnosis has converted me to a new reality; I have moved from a committed, self-righteous skeptic about the potential benefits of digital connectivity to an unabashed advocate for the under-appreciated ability of virtual spaces to help incarnate healing love in the lives of those who suffer. And with the zeal common to converts, I am on a mission to spread this message to any and all who will listen.

But sometimes it can be a tough sell, at least initially. Recently I was in Canada getting ready to testify to the gospel of the virtual body of Christ with a gathering of pastors. Before I spoke, I invited the ministers to introduce themselves in order to help me better understand their contexts for ministry. One clergy member offered a snarky greeting about how he *could not wait* to hear what I had to say about the value of thinking about the body of Christ *virtually*, because such a notion runs so counter to emphasis on the *physical* presence of the body of Christ, which we all know is what really matters, and that virtual presence is not just a lesser form of presence but is, in fact, detrimental to the church being the church.

I smiled at his impassioned opposition to virtual interaction. Before my diagnosis, his position was exactly my position; however, since my experience of being ministered to virtually in life-sustaining ways by the hands and feet of Christ, I'm out to convert others to notice, understand, and participate in the life-giving work of the virtual body of Christ.

A month after my time with the pastors in Canada, I received this message via e-mail from the one with the snarky greeting. He wrote:

> Yesterday, at the ordination of a colleague, as I have many times since your time with us in Winnipeg, I told them how your compelling presentation had inculcated in

9

me a *metanoia* with regards the whole notion of "the virtual body of Christ" which I had contemptuously dismissed before my Spirit-led encounter with you last month. It was your courage and poise that brought your message home to me and caused me to "turn about" when considering this subject. I thought it might be meaningful for you to know that the seeds you planted in the very short time you had to convince me have yielded a harvest in so many other people and places you will never know and I thought that would be an encouragement . . . that what you say, what you are living, your work . . . matters . . . and is making a difference.[5]

This story illustrates what the church is up against regarding our digital revolution: many committed Christian leaders lament, scoff at, and even dismiss those who proclaim the possibilities of ministry through these new virtual spaces. Because I proudly shared these views until I got sick and because I have had a conversion experience that has allowed me to see the potential in digitized communication to minister to those who suffer, I offer this book in hopes of facilitating more *metanoia* (a change of heart, spiritual conversion) and occasions to turn about negative opinions regarding the power of the virtual body of Christ to bring healing, hope, and light into the darkest times of our lives.

The experience of being enveloped by the virtual body of Christ also necessarily leads to a reconsideration of what it means to be a church in the twenty-first century. I'm with pastor and writer Jason Byassee when he proposes that Christians ought neither to reject our emerging digitized reality nor simply baptize it. Byassee instead frames Christian negotiation of the digital world as another dimension of Christ and culture, a dimension that calls for healthy appropriation and critical engagement by scholars and church leaders alike.[6] This book proposes a vision for how churches can appropriate and engage the digital tools available to us to more fully incarnate the body of Christ in our world today.

Chapter 1 includes a call to accept that the digital revolution is here to stay and to resist seeing ourselves as fully determined by or utterly captive to our new technology. Understanding the latest technological products as tools allows us to think more imaginatively about how we can utilize technology to help form connections and communities that will support one another through the toughest of times. Drawing on the work of sociologists who analyze the interplay of weak and strong ties in our social networks, I demonstrate how virtual networks are being utilized to foster both weak and strong ties that make transformational differences in the lives of those who suffer.

The second chapter returns to the first century, to the origins of the church, and traces how the Apostle Paul drew on ancient depictions of community as a body in order to imagine the Christian community as the body of Christ. The chapter highlights how Paul's use of the image was both distinctive and innovative, especially in his reversal of status amid the hierarchy of members within the body. In particular, Paul's vision of the weakest members being the most honorable in the body of Christ provides a radically different view of community than other prevailing views of the day. And even though Paul traveled only rarely to be physically present with the church communities throughout Asia Minor, he remained present with those communities *virtually* through his letters. In ways similar to the digital connectivity that fosters both weak and strong ties, Paul's membership in the body of Christ relied on weak and strong ties to make care possible for the weakest members of the body. And most vitally, it was the body of Christ as a *virtual* body that made actual care of the weakest not just possible but a top priority.

Building on the understanding that virtual communities, like the body of Christ, have significant material consequences, chapter 3 addresses both the centrality of the incarnation for Christian thought and practice as well as critiques by scholars within Christianity that the virtual world seriously threatens Christians' ability to live incarnationally and thus faithfully. Even as such critiques are worthy of serious consideration, this chapter proposes that by seeing virtual reality as *continuous* rather than *discontinuous* with embodied existence, it becomes clear that at times virtual interactions can be even more beneficial—and therefore incarnational—than face-to-face ones. The chapter concludes with a theology of incarnation for the digital age that identifies the ability of Christ's presence to expand in cruciform ways through virtual connectivity, able to reach those who suffer in ways not possible when limited to face-to-face contact.

After having fleshed out an incarnational theology that includes virtual as well as material spaces, chapter 4 explores the claim that, in the digital age, one of our most pressing problems is not lack of presence but instead being present to too many at the same time. This chapter explores ways of cultivating attention and practicing intentional presence with those who suffer and continues with a presentation of ways the church can play a pivotal, countercultural role in cultivating these spiritual practices. Using the biblical story of blind Bartimaeus from the Gospel of Mark, I propose a vision for the virtual body of Christ that stops and attends, as Jesus did, to those most in need of care, comfort, and healing.

With the theological foundation and the spiritual importance of the virtual body of Christ more fully fleshed out, the final chapter envisions an ecclesiology that moves beyond present pressures for churches to create effective digital strategies to imagining church as a community that utilizes digital connectivity in order to expand and deepen its understanding of how we relate to and care for one another, especially the weakest among us. At the same time, limitations of the virtual body of Christ are acknowledged for those whose illnesses or disabilities make use of digital devices difficult to impossible. The book concludes with a return to my experience with how online social networks of support encourage new thinking about the theological boundaries of the body of Christ.

For the past seven years, my family and I have been living with the burden of an advanced stage cancer diagnosis. And amid the worst days of life with cancer, we have been converted to the power of the virtual world to offer life-giving support and a healing presence that has helped us carry on. My hope is that readers making their way through this book will also be converted to the surprising ways that virtual connectivity can help us better care for one another. Even more, I hope that churches will continue to identify the digital revolution as one that offers new tools to help us better be the hands and feet of Christ in support of those who suffer. Won't you join me in proclaiming the good news of the virtual body of Christ?

SMS

Chapter 1
Imagine That

Our World Is the Virtual World

> *And that is what technology is, a tool. The roots of the word technology are in the Greek name for practical things that extend our human capacities. Some of our more famous technologies, the wheel, the printing press, have changed the world in unimaginably diverse ways. So too will our digital tools, with an emphasis on the unimaginable part. The tools will only be as good as the imaginations of the people that put them to use.*
>
> —T. V. Reed, *Digitized Lives*

It can be overwhelming to try to make sense of our increasingly digitized lives. New forms of virtual communication proliferate daily, leaving many of us bewildered as to how we will ever keep up. It is not overstating the case to say that digital means of communication are revolutionizing the way humans interact with one another as well as how we produce knowledge. In fact, this time of ever-changing digitization of our world is being called a "fourth revolution" that follows three previous human revolutions that changed the way we think, communicate, and interact: language, writing, and the printing press.[1] In this list of revolutions, human speech is the initial one, emerging before recorded history and making human beings the first—and thus far the only—species to describe and explain the world in which we live. Writing, the next revolution, came along much later, taking the codification of thought made possible in speaking and preserving it apart from any one particular speaker. The third revolution, movable type, was invented first in Asia in the ninth century but took quite a few centuries to be utilized frequently, likely due to the complexity of Asian writing systems.[2] The invention of the printing press in medieval Europe caught on more quickly and made it possible for texts to be distributed much more quickly and broadly than before. And in the twenty-first century, many deem the current technological sea change a digital revolution, one that makes possible near-instant gathering of information and communication with people both near and far.

While few of us living in the twenty-first century would want to imagine life without the products of the previous three revolutions, it is important to realize that such massive revolutions in communication have always caused consternation, worry, and upheaval as well as excitement, innovation, and transformation. With the invention of writing, for instance, Greek philosophers like Socrates worried that human capacity for memory would be fundamentally compromised, as people would simply rely on a text rather than on their own ability to memorize.[3] Even as evaluators of history see the invention of the printing press as an overwhelmingly positive development that revolutionized access to texts and increased literacy and access to knowledge, many learned people of the Middle Ages worried that mass production of printed materials would cheapen the craft of book making and, again, damage the ability of people to memorize and recite poetry, literature, and sacred stories. Other important technological innovations like the telegraph led cultural critics to lament the loss of people being oriented toward local communities and local events, as news from across the nation and eventually the world became available and often took precedent to what was happening in the neighborhood.[4] All these examples demonstrate that technological innovation changes us in unanticipated, sometimes destabilizing, and potentially threatening ways.

In terms of the digital revolution unfolding around us, we need not look far to see that consternation and worry over the implications of digitalization run high. Even though I have been converted to some of the positive, transformative uses of digital technology, I am not immune to such worries. On a macro level, I share concerns over the impact in places like the Democratic Republic of Congo where "conflict minerals" (like tin, tantalum, and tungsten, all needed for our ubiquitous devices) are mined at great human and environmental cost,[5] over the prevalence of smart phone use while driving,[6] and over the potential health risks (especially to children) of constant possession of electronic devices,[7] to name just a few. On the micro level, I continue to grow uncomfortable when people in restaurant booths near mine eat in silence as they scroll their phones or when parents ignore their children's sincere desire for interaction in favor of whatever is moving across the screen on their mobile device. Whether or not digital tools enhance or detract from meaningful interpersonal relationships continues to be debated. We know, for instance, that research suggests that Americans are growing increasingly isolated in terms of meaningful communal as well as personal connections, a trend that has been in place since the 1980s.[8] That feelings of so-cial isolation have been on the rise long before any of us went digital suggests that the emergence of the Internet does not bear sole (or even primary) responsibility for our sense of disconnection. Smaller families, more people living farther from extended families, declines in civic engagement, and less participation in religious communities all challenge well-established ways of being connected to one an-other. Yet for many critics of current technological trends, one common narrative is that the digital revolution exacerbates and amplifies such realities.

While concerns about technological revolutions go hand-in-hand with tech-nological innovation, some critics of the digital revolution insist that the impact of *this* revolution is distinctively problematic. Writer Nicholas Carr, author of *The Shallows: What the Internet Is Doing to Our Brains*, argues that unlike most other technologies, the Internet and our increasing addiction to it is causing us to lose touch with the "real world." In our relentless engagement with digital devices, our brains are being trained to constantly refocus our attention, flitting from one thing to another in "real life" just as we do online.[9] Other digital critics like soci-ologist James Davison Hunter insist that our current revolution is reshaping no-tions of intimacy, and not for the better.[10] I imagine most of us hear at least some truth in these critiques. Many of us likely have experienced the frustrating lack of focus when we multitask with e-mail, Facebook, a work document, and texting all at once. We have felt the challenges that 24/7 digital connectivity presents to the relationships with those we love the most. We are quite aware that liabilities exist in, with, and through the current digital revolution.

As we try to determine how new technology is altering our lives for better or for worse, it is important to resist adopting a simplistic version of *technologi-cal determinism* that avoids the complexity of the issue. To illustrate this point, take the example of online education and the potential problems with thinking about it within a deterministic framework. It is not enough, for instance, to in-sist that online education—simply because it is not conducted face-to-face—is inherently less effective than education that happens when people are physically together in the same space. We know from experience that bad teaching happens in face-to-face environments as well as in online ones. At the same time, it seems irresponsible to endorse online teaching and argue for its intrinsic superiority to face-to-face education simply because it utilizes the newest technology. Most of us also know from experience that it is entirely possible for in-person teaching to be knock-your-socks-off good even with minimal use of technology. Versions of both positive and negative technological determinism mistakenly argue that simply using the technology guarantees a particular outcome. Neither approach recognizes, however, that when technology is understood as a tool, its ability to help make lives better or worse depends on *how it is used*.

But critics like Carr caution against rejecting determinism too quickly in order to embrace a wholly *instrumentalist* view of technology, where technology is instead seen as a neutral artifact, completely dependent upon users to determine its influence. This view of technology tends to be the dominant one, Carr believes, because we want it to be true.[11] Looking broadly at how technology influences societies in which it is used, we can see that technology often does the shaping of individuals and communities alike, often much more than we would like to admit. Carr himself leans more toward a deterministic viewpoint, sounding the alarm that technology can and will alter even the way our brains work and encouraging us to resist going "gently into the future our computer engineers and software programmers are scripting for us."[12] Carr calls on all of us who use digital technology to develop more critical awareness of the ways new technologies are reshaping our lives so that we can resist what seems virtually inevitable.

Carr is far from the only one calling us to examine the technological scripts we're being handed along with our Wi-Fi passwords. Growing numbers of scholars and activists insist that technologies themselves are "inherently social and political."[13] New technologies do not simply come into being randomly; rather, they most often are created because entities like the government or businesses have actively supported and funded their inventions. Some groups that have been particularly vocal about the political nature of our technology are those who advocate for the rights of those who are disabled. Disability rights activists acknowledge that while technological innovations like the wheelchair have been liberating for people with mobility issues, "it is worth asking whether a more liberating form of mobility would exist for people who currently use wheelchairs if they constituted some of the most powerful members of society."[14] In other words, paying attention to what and how new technologies are created—and whose interests they serve or fail to serve—challenges the view that technology is "just a tool."

There is no doubt that the digital revolution we are currently living through is igniting change in virtually all dimensions of our lives. The Internet and digital technology are tools, yes, but tools accompanied by scripts and cultures influenced by political interests and ideologies beyond our control. And as Carr suggests, the debate between the determinists and the instrumentalists will likely never be resolved.[15] But even as we acknowledge that technologies come with ideological baggage, we also must realize that cultures—even ones with powerful ideological interests—are capable of change. Take American culture and its history of racism as just one example. While this issue is incredibly complex, requiring nuanced analysis to understand its insidious layers, my invoking of this example here is to point to places where powerful ideological agendas have not been able to prevent significant change. When Barack Obama was elected the first black president of the United States in 2008, for instance, Atlanta mayor Shirley Franklin declared, "Just a little more than ten years ago it was inconceivable to any of us that we would see an African American win a national party's ticket and then compete effectively. It's mind-boggling."[16] Anyone familiar with American legal and political culture knows that white racism has long been a central and defining feature of those cultures. Obama's election most certainly has not brought about an end to racism within American legal and political cultures; nevertheless, the two-term election of a black president is a striking illustration of how even cultures steeped in powerful ideologies are *capable* of change.

Even as the Internet and the tools of the digital revolution come wrapped in potentially powerful cultures, then, it is still possible to affect how they impact us by how we choose to participate in these cultures. Therefore, while our current digital revolution is capable of increasing disconnection, disengagement, and isolation within and among groups of people, if we're intentional and imaginative about how we use it, digitized Internet technology can also enhance, deepen, and even transform our connections with one other. I know. My conversion story testifies to the surprising power of connection I have found via online networks since the onset of my illness. I will testify again about the healing power made possible by digital technology after we explore emerging perspectives on the capability of new technology to create and sustain meaningful online connections.

Strong and Weak Ties Exist Both Online and Offline

While it is the case that there now are more cell phones than people in the world,[17] it is also the case that, as of the year 2014, 4.4 billion people across the globe were not yet connected to the Internet.[18] Access to and participation in the digital revolution remains restricted by scripts and cultures that privilege certain geography, abilities, and types of communities over others. Therefore, we must not pretend that the World Wide Web is actually worldwide or that our imaginings of this virtual connectivity have the capacity yet for literal universal reach. At the same time, even if Google executive Eric Schmidt is incorrect in his prediction that everyone on the globe will be connected to the Internet by 2020,[19] the digital revolution shows no signs of slowing down. Our world is being altered; we're becoming increasingly connected digitally and virtually. Our task as individuals, and our task in communities like the church, is to think imaginatively about how digital technology can enhance our lives, especially in its potential to help counter the sense of isolation and disconnection that threaten to persist in this digital age.

One way to explore how we can utilize digital technology to enhance a culture of interconnection with other human beings is to listen to discussions by sociologists and others about whether or not digitized social networks are capable of being "strong tie networks," that is, networks of people we trust who can help us weather change and the uncertainty that comes with it.[20] All of us live within webs of social networks composed of both strong and weak ties. Since the rise of the Internet, and especially since the "Arab Spring" movements toward democracy in 2011 and the recent emergence of the Black Lives Matter movement in the United States, scholars, journalists, and others have been debating whether or not it is possible to create online social networks strong enough to transform the ways we relate to one another and organize our communities.[21] On one side of the debate are social critics like Malcolm Gladwell, who argued that "the revolution will not be tweeted," a position that nurtures skepticism of Web-based social media and their "weak-tie environments."[22] When assessing the capacity of social media to create strong ties among individuals and communities, Gladwell insists, "The platforms of social media are built around weak ties. Twitter is a way of following (or being followed by) people you may never have met. Facebook is a tool for efficiently managing your acquaintances, for keeping up with people you would not otherwise be able to stay in touch with."[23] While sociologists have long acknowledged that weak ties are a given—even necessary—component of our social networks,[24] Gladwell gives voice to a common concern regarding the types of relationships being formed online: that networks created through social media are primarily weak-tie environments and thus incapable of supporting strong-tie networks or, for his purposes, instigating meaningful political or social change. Critics continue to build on Gladwell's concerns, derisively referring to online organizing around social and political causes as "click activism" or "slacktivism,"[25] where the strength of the ties amounts to little more than clicking "like" at the end of a post that professes something similar to what we already believe.

If Gladwell's analysis is correct, why would the church want to spend more time utilizing digital tools when the end goal is to build strong-tie environments that foster trust, support, and healing around the broken and hurting in our midst? Theologian Stanley Hauerwas makes clear that when the church is being the church, it should be a strong-tie environment made up of people "who have learned how to be faithful to one another by our willingness to be present, with all our vulnerabilities, to one another."[26] If, then, the body of Christ is called to be present to one another in and out of pain, don't we need networks built primarily on strong ties and, therefore, networks that are primarily offline?

A potent counterexample to Gladwell's skepticism about social change being brought about through ties made via social media is the emergent Black Lives Matter movement. This movement began on social media in the aftermath of the acquittal of George Zimmerman in the summer of 2013 for the killing of unarmed black teen Trayvon Martin. Oakland community organizer Alicia Garza wrote a Facebook post in response to the verdict entitled "A Love Note to Black People" calling on black Americans to "get organized" and "fight back." Garza concluded her post by saying, "Our Lives Matter, Black Lives Matter." Patrisse Cullors, another community organizer in California who is Facebook friends with Garza, responded to the post with the hashtag "#BlackLives Matter," and a new organization was born.[27] This movement emerging via social media is helping write a new chapter in the history of the struggle for civil rights in this country, according to historian Herbert Ruffin. Comprising both strong and weak ties, the Black Lives Matter movement seems to be tweeting at least glimpses of revolution, as their demands to meet in 2015 with 2016 Democratic presidential hopefuls Hilary Clinton and Bernie Sanders were fulfilled and they were able to discuss how their campaigns can better address racial injustices and police reform. The movement's influence in specific actions across the nation has also been visible in 2015, from the Confederate flag being removed from the South Carolina statehouse to recent student protests over racial problems at the University of Missouri leading to the resignation of the university president.[28] These actions, promoted and supported by the Black Lives Matter movement, seem far afield from the slacktivism decried by those who reject the possibility of meaningful online organizing for change.

Viewing online networks as weak and therefore ineffective, then, neglects several significant insights about how social networks operate. First, strong and weak ties are not opposing forces but instead work in complementary ways within social networks; second, the ties that bind are often fluid, with strong ties sometimes growing weaker and weak ties sometimes growing stronger; and third, weak ties play vital roles in social networks, expanding and making room for new insights, new opportunities, and new ways of interacting. While Gladwell casts weak ties in a negative light and advocates for networks dominated instead by strong ties, sociologist Mark Granovetter argued decades ago that weak ties work in tandem with strong ties and should not be dismissed as insignificant or simply inferior to strong ties. His research examined the interplay of strong and weak ties in how subjects in his study came to interview for and get hired at a new job. Granovetter showed that it is most often people's weak ties that link them to new job opportunities, and he argued that weak ties provide bridges to new information and social networks outside one's primary (strong-tie) networks.[29]

Decades after the publication of Granovetter's results, sociologists continue to expand on the value of weak ties as not only being useful in their own right but also being helpful for their ability to reinforce strong ties within a given network. So even if weak ties are prevalent in cyberspace, this does not mean that virtual networks are without strong ties. In the Black Lives Matter movement, strong-tie connections between community organizers in California became catalysts for a movement that spread rapidly through the weak and strong ties of social media. This example reinforces new thinking emerging out of the growing field of technosociology, where sociologists like Zeynep Tufekci propose that social media connections are just as capable as face-to-face connections to foster strong ties:

> [The] Internet bolsters strong ties directly and indirectly. Directly, because the Internet allows for more frequent, trivial "ambient" communication and that is the bedrock of strong-tie formation. All those tweets about what you had for breakfast that everyone makes fun of? A lot of research shows that if you record ordinary people's conversations with their close friends and family and you will find that this is exactly what they do—talk about the mundane rhythms of life.[30]

Tufekci's point is that in twenty-first-century North American society, where people increasingly structure their lives in ways that seem to encourage disconnection (see the above discussion about Americans' growing sense of social isolation), online social networks with high populations of weak ties may actually contribute to the formation of strong ties that foster connection and trust.

Further evidence that Granovetter's thesis about the strength of weak ties also has relevance for online social networks is seen in how people utilize weak ties online to gather information on and receive support for health issues. Take blogger Mary Evelyn's story of bringing her newborn son with spina bifida (a congenital defect of the spine where part of the spinal cord is exposed through a gap in the backbone) home from hospital and growing increasingly concerned with his abnormal breathing patterns. Calls to the pediatrician and nurses at the spina bifida clinic yielded calm attempts to reassure Mary Evelyn that such breathing was nothing to be concerned about. Still anxious, she turned to online support groups for parents of children with spina bifida. These weak-tie connections validated her concerns, with one stranger suggesting she take a video of her sleeping infant and bring it into the clinic for the staff to watch, which she did. After viewing the video, the medical staff immediately admitted her son to the hospital, where he underwent surgery for a tracheotomy. All this she writes in her blog post entitled "The Time the Internet Saved My Son's Life." Mary Evelyn testifies to the potentially powerful value of weak ties online, ones that bring with them new information that can literally help save lives. She writes, "Strangers on the Internet knew my son was in danger before the doctors did—and I think that's kind of amazing."[31] And just as Tufekci suggests, these ties that start out as weak sometimes transform into strong ties. "It takes a village to raise a child," Mary Evelyn admits, "but it takes a large metropolitan area to raise a child with spina bifida. I found my people online."[32] Those other parents of children with spina bifida have become strong ties for Mary Evelyn and her family, forming a vital network of information, support, and assistance in times of anxiety and worry over a newborn's health.

Thus it is the case that growing numbers of participants in and analysts of the digital revolution believe that strong-tie environments do exist in cyberspace and that they can be created virtually. Howard Rheingold, author of *The Virtual Community: Homesteading on the Electronic Frontier*, insists that virtual networks can be as strong as ones that meet face-to-face. He suggests that "the technology that makes virtual communities possible has the potential to bring enormous leverage to ordinary citizens at relatively little cost—intellectual leverage, social leverage, and most important, political leverage. But the technology will not in itself fulfill that potential; this latent technical power must be used intelligently and deliberatively by an informed population."[33] While there is certainly much to lament about online interactions by seemingly uninformed populations, Rheingold returns to that pivotal point: it depends upon how the technology is used.

The Conversion Story Continues: Strong-Tie Connections That Deepen and Heal through Virtual Networks

As social media sites become more ubiquitous in our lives, it is important to realize that they are increasingly used to communicate with the strong ties that populate our networks.[34] We see posts about an aunt and uncle's anniversary celebration, photos of a friend's hospital visit after slipping on the ice, a status update on our own child's romantic relationships, all of which facilitate ways of staying up-to-date with what is going on in the lives of people we care about. And there are times when social media networks allow us to deepen those ties, even transform relationships in ways that would have been nearly impossible without the help of digital connectivity. In the opening chapter, I shared stories of prayers for healing being done on my behalf by family and friends from Jerusalem and India to St. Paul and Oakland, California. But there is another story of phenomenal gift giving made possible by virtual connections that involves the making of a quilt. This story played an important role in my conversion to understanding that digital technology can be used to bring people together in ways that can support—even contribute to healing for—those who suffer.

It is not hard to imagine ways in which a sudden diagnosis of a serious illness can disrupt and destabilize not just the person with the illness and that person's family but also the wider community of family and friends who care about that person as well. The suddenness in December 2008 with which I went from being a healthy, active woman in my early forties to a person confined to the house and unable even to dress myself was difficult for those who care about me to witness, understand, and accept. Family and close friends wanted to help, but it was often unclear just what help should look like when lives are radically altered and the future is draped in uncertainty.

A close friend of mine was one of many who brought food to our house in those first weeks after the diagnosis. Even so, she wanted to do more. She prayed for guidance. Then one day, she has told us, a clear message came to her: that she should make a quilt for our family. This is a friend who pays attention to such messages, so she used my CaringBridge website to develop her own virtual network via e-mail, explaining in her messages that she was on a mission to make a quilt for us and inviting people to contact her if they wanted to participate. This friend then sent quilt squares in the mail, met people clandestinely in coffee shops to hand off more patterns and scraps of cloth, and hosted secret quilting nights at her house during the entire summer of 2009. All the while this friend was deepening connections between and among dozens of people whose only initial connection was with me.

In fall of that year, our family was told an elaborate tale to get us to the quilting friend's house one Saturday afternoon. We were ushered into the house to find our extended family, friends, neighbors, and coworkers waiting to surprise us. In the middle of the living room, on a wooden frame, sat an exquisite quilt flanked by friends and family armed with needles and thread. The kitchen was filled with many more people who were preparing a feast for the event. My daughters, my husband, and I were utterly baffled at this assembly of people who were for some unknown reason gathered on our behalf. It took our friend's explanation and a full afternoon of conversation with those in attendance to start to grasp what had been going on for the previous several months. Our strong ties of family and friends, we slowly came to realize, had been making not just a phenomenal gift of comfort for us during this traumatic time in our lives, but they had also been forming new strong ties with one another. The gift and the ties, it was stunning to realize, were all made possible by the virtual network created in the wake of my illness.

This part of my conversion story illustrates not just how virtual network can support strong ties and encourage new formations of strong ties among weak ties, but it also provides evidence of how virtual networks do not exist merely in virtual space; they exist in both virtual and physical spaces, the virtual connecting in concrete ways to the "real" (material) world. Every night that my husband and I wrap ourselves in the quilt made by those who love, care, and pray for us, we are physically covered by a tangible sign of all of those who surround and support us as we walk this journey with cancer. Words cannot adequately convey what a gift that is. It's the stuff conversions are made of.

What Language Shall We Borrow for Living in Both the Offline and Online Worlds Simultaneously?

To say that both strong and weak ties exist in online as well as offline networks reinforces the point made by digital culture scholar T. V. Reed: that we are always in the "real world" even when we're also online.[35] Unfortunately, the language we use to talk about the digital revolution often reinforces a negative view of Internet cultures and the effects they have on all of us who participate in them. Take the word *cyberspace*, a term that comes from William Gibson's 1984 science fiction novel *Neuromancer* that has persisted in popularity in conversations about the digital revolution. Gibson himself offers this cheery assessment of cyberspace, calling it "a consensual hallucination" of billions of users. More pragmatically speaking, Gibson explains that cyberspace is also a "graphic representation of data abstracted from the banks of every computer in the human system."[36] That the term comes from a story of a dystopian future of computer hacking leaves those who want to highlight what we might *gain* from using digital technology looking for other terms with less negative connotations. But Reed, who sees great potential for digital technology to enhance our collective lives, suggests the term *cyberspace* can be useful in that its reference to *space* reminds us that our engagement with digital domains is always done spatially, with all of us accessing such domains from particular devices in specific locations, all of which depend upon an increasingly vast physical infrastructure of servers, data centers, and more.[37] In continuing to use the term, Reed offers a slight modification, preferring the plural *cyberspaces* to the singular form of the word in order to indicate the inherent plurality of sites, domains, and locations utilized by the millions of people who interact in, with, and through the Internet.

As is likely apparent by now, I find the term *virtual* to be a workable metaphor for thinking and talking about our new age of digitalization. Virtual reality, it is important to note, has come to refer not just to digital interconnections in general but also to virtual realities (VRs) more generally, that is, realities created digitally for entertainment, training, and therapeutic purposes. Military training utilizes VR simulators to prepare soldiers for combat, while the gaming industry creates elaborate VRs for gamers to inhabit. Linguistically speaking *virtual reality* (VR) or *virtual life* (VL) is typically contrasted with "actual" reality or *real life* (RL), thus encouraging the bifurcated view that being online or connected digitally is utterly distinct from *real* or embodied reality. But thinking of *virtual reality* as diametrically opposed to *real* or "offline" reality carries with it a set of problems, because as Reed points out, virtual reality is a continuation of real reality:

> It is important to take that illusion of virtuality [of the virtual world] seriously; it is
> to some degree a new kind of experience. But it is also not wholly new (whenever we

read a novel we also enter a virtual world, just not a digitally delivered one). Part of studying virtual worlds should be to remind users that they are never just in a virtual world, but also always in a real one too.[38]

Reed's observation that being present online never actually negates our offline existence is also reinforced by the work of Tom Boellstorff, an anthropologist who conducted an influential ethnographic study of Second Life, a virtual 3-D world created in 2003 where users create avatars and participate in a virtual society. Boellstorff no doubt would appreciate Reed's comparison between the virtual worlds of cyberspaces and the virtual worlds of novels, for he argues that "it is in being virtual that we are human; since it is human 'nature' to experience life through the prism of culture, human being has always been virtual being."[39] In other words, virtual reality—even in its most recent digitized form—is inextricably bound up with what it means to be human; it is in our nature to utilize technology (the pen, the book, the Internet) to extend versions of ourselves and our world beyond our physical limits.

As far as human beings as a species are concerned, then, virtual realities are nothing new. But as Reed reminds us in the quote above, it is worth considering the distinctive shapes of virtual reality as they pertain to our current digital age. In his attempts at defining what a virtual world is, Boellstorff points to a common definition of the term *virtual* as "almost" and suggests we might think about the definition of *virtual* as approaching what is actual or real without ever actually arriving there. While thinking about Second Life and other virtual worlds as almost-worlds might well be appropriate, I am less sure *almost* works as a modifier when applied to terms like *virtual conversations* or *virtual interactions* when referring to digital communication. A conversation with my daughter via text about her day at school and when she plans to be home is not qualitatively different than if I were to talk to her in person about those same topics. Some may want to object to my viewing a conversation via text as a real conversation, insisting, perhaps, that the tone of her voice as well as the nonverbal cues I would get if we were to converse in person simply cannot be duplicated virtually. But I would counter by highlighting first that my daughter's creative use of emojis goes a long way in giving me a pretty accurate sense of how she is doing, and second, that having an in-person conversation, we all know, is no guarantee of having a *real* conversation. I support anthropologists Heather Horst and Daniel Miller in their opposition to assessments about our current digital revolution that imply that our virtual interactions have "rendered us less human, less authentic or more mediated."[40] It simply is the case that virtual conversations can be—and often are—real conversations. On this point Boellstorff also agrees. Even as he wants to be clear that there are important distinctions between the virtual world of Second Life and the real world where he physically resides and works, his main point is that we have not yet found fully adequate ways to speak about the distinctiveness of each of those worlds. For Boellstorff, the term *real world* is an "imprecise antonym" to *virtual world* because it implies that technology makes life less real, when what is the case is that our virtual worlds and virtual connections with one another are in many ways "just as real as our rl [real life] ones."[41] So even though there are currently imprecise terms to demarcate the differences, it is nevertheless the case that virtual spaces, worlds, and connections offer us opportunities to consider our humanity anew, and to reconfigure possibilities for "place-making, subjectivity, and community."[42]

In light of the abundant potential within the virtual for creating meaning, it is also important to take note that the term *virtual* has its roots in the Latin word *virtus* (not distant from the term *virtue*), which suggests excellence, potency, efficacy. As we consider how we might utilize digital tools to better imagine ways to connect with and care for one another, I want us to continue to imagine—even as we're clear-eyed about the ways in which digital technology can encourage disconnection—ways in which digital tools can help facilitate efficacious connections to mitigate the sense of despair and hopelessness that threatens all of us at the worst of times. Utilized effectively, virtual connectivity can help us better attend to the hurt that fills our lives.

But just as we grow comfortable with using the term *virtual* to talk about dimensions of our lives that are online, we are reminded of the ever-changing nature of the revolution in digital technology and how continuous rapid change demands that the language we use to talk about it continues to evolve. At present, it is the case that increasing numbers of us no longer "go online"; instead, we are already there most waking hours of each day. Our smart phones constantly offer up headline news stories, weather updates, text messages, and the latest from Facebook, Twitter, Instagram, and more. To more fully capture this emerging reality of being continuously connected, technological language is evolving to talk not just of *virtual reality* but also of *augmented reality* (AR). Augmented Reality.org defines AR as "an emerging technology that digitizes interaction with the physical world."[43] Google glasses are not quite here yet, but for millions of smart-phone users, apps augment our eating, shopping, exercising, and devotional experiences—in short, our way of interacting with virtually (pun intended) all aspects of the physical world.

And while Nicholas Carr's and others' hand wringing over the loss of connections to the real world definitely is worth paying attention to, we cannot ignore the ways in which VR and AR are enhancing real human lives. VRs created for surgeons to use for training purposes help eliminate what professor of surgery Donn Spight calls "learning by random opportunity."[44] Today, atypical or rare physical conditions can be created virtually, permitting medical students and resident surgeons to develop skills (and confidence) in techniques and procedures without someone's life or health on the line.[45] With respect to augmented reality, scientists are beginning to harness applications of AR to stimulate the brain in Parkinson's patients in order to improve cognitive functions and mobility.[46] For growing numbers of people with serious medical issues, digitally enhanced realities are improving the lives of those who would otherwise suffer much more greatly.

Even as we acknowledge that emerging technology has the potential to decrease suffering and prolong life, it is also important to attend to ways that our participation in cyberspaces is altering our conceptions of the world and our place in it. Debates arise over how much digitization is too much. Whether and how the body of Christ is and can be present virtually in the twenty-first century with those who suffer is a critical question that invites serious theological reflection. And in order to consider the future, we should also reconsider the past and return to the origins of Christian communities and the social networks and cultures of connection envisioned in those earliest communities of faith. Locating resources in the first century and beyond for thinking about *how* to be the body of Christ will help us move forward in utilizing contemporary technological tools to better be the types of communities Christians are called to embody in and for the world.

Part Two

Virtually There:
The Body of Christ
as a Virtual Body

Chapter 2
The Body of Christ Has Always Been and Will Always Be a Virtual Body

Christ has no body but yours,
No hands, no feet on earth but yours,
Yours are the eyes with which he looks
Compassion on this world,
Yours are the feet with which he walks to do good,
Yours are the hands, with which he blesses all the world.
Yours are the hands, yours are the feet,
Yours are the eyes, you are his body.
Christ has no body now but yours.

—St. Teresa of Avila, "Christ Has No Body"

Widely attributed to St. Teresa of Avila (1515–1582), this medieval prayer casts in stark, fleshy imagery how followers of Christ are called to *be* the body of Christ in a broken, hurting world. Christ is present *virtually*, through the bodies and the actions of his followers. In this prayer, St. Theresa riffs off biblical imagery offered by the Apostle Paul who utilizes images of the body to help the early churches envision what kind of community they are called to be: "Now you are the body of Christ and individually members of it" (1 Cor 12:27 NRSV). Just as it is the case in the medieval prayer, so it is for Paul: that members of the body of Christ are commissioned to attend especially to those who are broken and hurting. "Instead, the parts of the body that people think are the weakest are the most necessary. The parts of the body that we think are less honorable are the ones we honor the most. . . . If one part suffers, all the parts suffer with it" (1 Cor 12:22-3a, 26a). Embodying Christ's love and care to those who suffer is for Paul—as well as for St. Teresa—a thoroughgoing, embodied, materially based task. Let us turn now to how and why Paul utilizes body imagery in his letters to ancient churches and to the ways in which a deeper understanding of his relationship with other members of the body of Christ can enhance our contemporary vision of what it means to be the body of Christ today.

To better understand Paul's imagery of the body and his relationship with the ancient churches in Corinth, Rome, and beyond, it is important to look first at the wider context of Paul's life story. The biblical narrative tells of the birth of Paul (then known as "Saul") in the Roman city of Tarsus, where Greek culture mixed with Roman structures of government (Acts 22:3). He was raised as a Jew (Phil 3:5) and educated under the tutelage of a highly respected Jewish leader (Acts 22:3). Prior to following Jesus, he also claimed membership in the Jewish Pharisean sect, a group with strict adherence to Jewish law and customs, and Paul reports in his letters on his initial role as persecutor of the followers of Jesus (Phil 3:6). The defining moment of his life came when he was traveling the road to Damascus and was confronted by a "light from heaven" and an accompanying voice that asked, "Saul, Saul, why are you harassing me?" When Paul asked the identity of the one speaking, the response he received was "I am Jesus, whom you are harassing" (Acts 9:4-5). After this encounter, Paul interpreted the vision as a command to cease persecuting the followers of Jesus and to proclaim the gospel message to the Gentiles (Gal 1:11-18).

For much of the history of the Common Era, Christian interpretations of Paul have characterized this vision on the road to Damascus as his conversion from Judaism to Christianity, claiming also that his conversion confirms the truth of Christianity over against the false vision of Judaism. More recently, however, biblical scholars claim that during Paul's life, there was not yet any well-defined "Christianity" to which to convert and therefore stress instead the continuities between Paul's identity as a Jew and his newer identity as a follower of Jesus.[1] While the degree to which Paul remains a Jew continues to be debated, there is considerably more agreement about the fact that Paul spent the rest of his life traveling among fledgling churches in the Mediterranean and Asia Minor, giving shape to the core convictions and practices of this new religious movement that is at once closely related to but also distinct from its Jewish roots. Because of his outspoken commitment to this emerging Jesus movement—a movement that Roman rulers found threatening during the time of Jesus and continued to find threatening in Paul's time—Paul was himself persecuted and imprisoned for his commitment to this new movement. The biblical account of Paul's life does not contain concrete information about his death, but second-century church leaders attest to his martyrdom.[2] This is the life of the one who sets the tone for Christian belief and practice more than perhaps any other single individual.

While the story of Paul the church planter, leader, and visionary is dramatic and fascinating in its own right, the focus of this chapter is on Paul's role as leader of the newly forming body of Christ, how his use of this image shaped his relationships with fellow members of the body, and what aspects of Paul's vision for the social network of the church might inform contemporary imaginings of the body of Christ in a digital age. While the question of whether and how the church needs reimaging continues to be a hot topic in twenty-first-century Christianity, biblical scholar James Thompson voices concern over "the near absence from the discussion [over how to reinvent the church] of Paul, the one who shaped [these] communities more than anyone else we know."[3] In thinking about how to shape communities of faith to be the hands and feet of Christ into the future, then, it is vital to return to the original visionary of the social network imagined as the body of Christ.

After experiencing the life-altering vision on the road to Damascus, Paul stopped persecuting followers of Jesus and began traveling extensively throughout the Roman Empire, participating in—and forming new—fledgling communities of those same followers. Scholars emphasize how Paul introduced a new model of community into the Greco-Roman world, one that often separated its members from their families, their tribes, or their civic communities "and brought them together with those whom they did not choose."[4] While Paul employed a variety of images to help these newly formed communities envision what it meant to be a community united in Christ, the organic image of the church as a body is one of most enduring and intriguing. Paul developed this particular image most extensively in his first letter to the church at Corinth. As is suggested in Acts 18, Paul stayed with the Corinthians for over a year, preaching and teaching and getting to know the community well. During the first century CE, Corinth was one of the largest and most important cities in ancient Greece because it served as a major center of trade between Asia and Western Europe. Even though most of Paul's converts were Greek, there is evidence that some were also Jewish (1 Cor 7:18-19), and that the Corinthian Christians lived in a diverse city with people from a variety of backgrounds. After about eighteen months of living with the community in Corinth, Paul set sail for Syria to continue his work with other churches, leaving the Corinthian church to continue on without his own physical presence among them.

Paul headed from Corinth to Ephesus and, while there, received reports of disagreement within the Corinthian community (cf. 1 Cor 1:11). The new converts in Corinth were wrestling with what their new identity as followers of Christ meant for their own internal community dynamics as well as what the relationship between their community and the wider society should look like. Internally, some deep divisions were forming over divergent interpretations of issues like marriage versus singleness, sexual norms, and proper use of spiritual gifts, as well as questions over Paul's authority in relationship to their community. And Paul, at that point far away with no plans of returning any time soon, "[made] use of the most relevant format of engagement,"[5] the letter, to communicate with this church he had come to love and was committed to leading. Based on Paul's words in 1 Corinthians 5:9, we know that what we today call the first letter to the Corinthians is actually *not* the first letter Paul sent to Corinth. Estimates are that Paul wrote at least four letters to the church at Corinth;[6] therefore, what we now call the first letter to the Corinthians is actually just one part of a much longer back-and-forth exchange between Paul and the Corinthian community, an exchange in which Paul offers guidance, rebuke, and instruction for what it means to live as a community devoted to Christ.

As an educated man of his time, Paul draws on resources from the ancient cultures he was a part of in order to communicate his vision of what it means to be a community that follows Christ. Even as Paul utilizes images, resources, and formats of the ancient Greco-Roman world, however, he also synthesizes them to create something new and distinctive for the time. For example, it is clear that Paul was familiar with letter-writing conventions of the ancient world. He begins his letter to the Corinthians (as he begins many of his letters) with an expected salutation, "Grace to you and peace from God our Father and the Lord Jesus Christ" (1 Cor 1:3), but as writer and scholar of Christian spirituality Elizabeth Drescher points out, here Paul combines a standard Greek salutation (*chairein*) with the theological term for grace (*charis*) as well as the Jewish greeting of peace (*shalom*) all into one greeting.[7] The Corinthians who heard this letter read aloud likely understood that Paul was riffing off both Gentile and Jewish traditions while at the same time utilizing common rhetorical conventions for his own purposes. "He plays with language," Drescher writes, "in a way that allows him to bridge an ethnic divide that would have seemed impossible in strictly social terms. In doing so, he gives the Corinthians language for a common faith without erasing their ethnic distinctiveness."[8] But identifying markers like language, ethnicity, and social class held powerful sway at Paul's time just as they do in ours.

So Paul turns to salient images and metaphors to help communicate his vision for what it means to be this new community that sees itself as unified in Christ despite the many differences that threaten to separate members of the community from one another.

In this Corinthian context of ongoing debates and long-simmering divisions about a whole host of issues, why does Paul utilize the image of a body in his quest to help this community understand itself as church? First of all, imaging the cosmos or the state as a body was a widespread practice in the ancient world and one that would have come readily to mind for Paul.[9] Historian of ancient Christianity Margaret Mitchell documents how the metaphor of the body was used in ancient political literature to show the need for cooperation among all members of a community. She also notes that the image was often utilized to counteract factionalism.[10] In Paul's letter to his "brothers and sisters" in Corinth, his reliance on body imagery is no doubt used for similar reasons. He appeals to the Corinthians that they should all be in agreement, with no divisions, and "united in the same mind and the same purpose" (1 Cor 1:10 NRSV). Like invocations of body imagery for political and social reasons, Paul's use of such imagery in the letter to the Corinthians also affirms the necessity of the various members seeing themselves as fitting together in a single community: "So the eye can't say to the hand, 'I don't need you,' or in turn, the head can't say to the feet, 'I don't need you'" (1 Cor 12:21). These images of the church as a body where every member has its place would have been an image—and a message—members of the Corinthian community had heard before.

Once again, however, Paul draws on familiar images and conventions and then transforms them into something new and distinctive. According to New Testament scholar Michelle Lee, invoking the image of state or society as a body often was done in the ancient world to reinforce the belief that a natural fellowship already exists among human beings. Stoic philosophy of the time affirmed that there was a natural, preexisting bond between people even before they came together to form community; therefore, people are called upon to acknowledge that, just like parts of a body, they are all related to one another in an organic way.[11] Paul invokes the image of the body, then, not just to counter the anticommunal behavior of some members of the Corinthian church by highlighting such fellowship,[12] but also to emphasize that what individual members consider to be in their self-interest "must be considered in light of their participation in the whole."[13] In fact, as Lee notes, Paul insists that self-understanding of the followers of Jesus can no longer be limited to a vision of oneself as an individual. The whole body cannot be a single member (1 Cor 12:17); instead, persons must see themselves in relationship to the other parts (eye, nose, mouth) in order to be able to exist as a body.[14]

This letter is presenting a vision of being a body that required significant re-socialization for the Corinthians, a group where gender, class, education, familial status, or status as a slave were just some of the factors that determined a person's standing and worth within the community. Paul writes that within the body of Christ, "none of you will become arrogant by supporting one of us against the other" (1 Cor 4:6b). As readers familiar with Paul's correspondence to the Corinthians already know, however, what Paul writes in other parts of the letter can be interpreted as contradicting this bold egalitarian vision. Debates persist as to whether the admonition in chapter 11 that women cover their heads in church because man "is the image and glory of God" while woman is "man's glory" (1 Cor 11:7) should be viewed primarily as a statement intended to subordinate women, or as a proposal to follow the social custom of virtuous women cover-ing their heads in public, or even as indicative of Paul's attempt to eliminate the status that came from the elaborateness of wealthy women's hairstyles of the time.[15] Regarding chapter 14's insistence that women be silent and subordinate in churches (1 Cor 11:34), there are those who believe it is a later, non-Pauline addition while others propose that the incongruence of the passage with the dominant vision of equality among the members of the body of Christ indicates Paul's inability as a person of his time to fully embrace the radical nature of the church as Christ's body.[16] Even though different clothing standards for women and men are present in chapter 11, it is worth pointing out that in that same chapter Paul finds it unremarkable that women as well as men are praying or prophesying (1 Cor 11:5).[17] Tacit approval of such public proclamations stands in direct conflict with Paul's admonition for women to be silent in church (1 Cor 14:34). While such tensions persist within the text, it is nevertheless the case that Paul's vision of the body of Christ in chapter 12 imagines the church as operating differently than does the wider society, where social status translates into a rank-ing of some individuals being viewed as more important than others. Paul's use of body imagery in 1 Corinthians makes the point repeatedly that each member has its own particular role and is dependent on the workings of every other part, inextricably bound to the sense of the body in its entirety.

Another point of divergence from conventional applications in Paul's utiliza-tion of body imagery to conceptualize the church is that the diversity of members within the body is not cast in opposition to its necessary unity. In his explanation of the variety of spiritual gifts in 1 Corinthians 12:4-11 (similarly described in Rom 12:3-8 as well), Paul insists that the diversity of gifts of the Spirit are given by God "for the common good" (1 Cor 12:7). That the listing of the charismata occurs just before the passage on the diversity and mutual reliance of each body part on one another makes visible what theologian Guillermo Hansen calls the "vulnerable interdependence" among all members of the body. Differences, then, are not cause for division but the provision for unity.[18]

Perhaps the way in which Paul's use of the image of the church as a body departs most significantly from society or the state imagined as a body is the way in which he first levels and then reverses the hierarchical relationship among the members of the body. Ancient invocations of body imagery typically presented the head as the ruling part, which frequently led to the head being deemed more necessary than other parts. As Lee explains, philosophers of the day were known to utilize body imagery in order to facilitate "cessation of strife through acceptance of one's place in the body."[19] Paul's use of body imagery in 1 Corinthians chapter 12, by contrast, presents the Corinthian community with a surprising reversal of status. Because the Corinthians are called upon to have the mind of Christ (1 Cor 2:16), they are henceforth called upon to perceive status differently than the ruling philosophies of the day. Acting as Christ acts, Paul proclaims, means that the weakest and least honorable among them deserve the greatest attention and place of honor (1 Cor 12:22-3). Even though social and political uses of body imagery at the time encouraged members of the body to sympathize with other members' suffering as well, Paul's insistence that the weakest members of the body are to be viewed as the top priority stands in startling contrast to the prevailing view of the hierarchy that exists within the body, highlighting the countercultural nature of Paul's vision for what it means to be the church. In addition, since the city of Corinth was a restored colony of Rome, it is also the case that Paul is enacting this reversal of status within an imperial context.[20] To call the community in Corinth "the body of Christ" that proclaims Jesus as Lord, then, counters a culture that proclaims that Caesar is lord, where Caesar is seen as ruler and head of the body. Once again, it is clear that Paul's application of the body metaphor to the church "deeply disrupts the smooth flow of the social hegemonic networks" of the time.[21]

Furthermore, it also can be argued that Paul's reversal of conventional ways of imagining hierarchy within the body is about more than just reversing the status quo. The reversal applies, Lee explains, not just to the Corinthian community but also to Christ and his way of living that led to the cross. Seeing those who are hurting as the most significant members of the body "is a fundamental and paradoxical principle that goes to the heart of the gospel and the nature of eschatological existence."[22] This means that Paul's understanding of the church as the body of Christ is aligned with the view of God's solidarity through the cross with those who suffer most. This privileging of the weakest within the community is what New Testament scholar Michael Gorman refers to as Paul's vision of a "cruciform hierarchy."[23] And in order for God's promised vision of a city where there's no more crying, no more dying (Rev 21) to be glimpsed in the here and now, God in Christ—and those who become members of the body of Christ thereafter—turns the focus toward the weakest members of the body. Indeed, Paul insists that it is God's arrangement of the body (1 Cor 12:24) that promotes care by the entire church of members who need it most, effectively foreshadowing what life looks like in the New Jerusalem.[24] What Paul offers here is nothing short of a total recasting of what it means to be human[25] in light of one's membership in the body of Christ.

After he paints a picture of how various parts of the body work together in 1 Corinthians 12:12-26, Paul then moves on to identify the Corinthians explicitly as Christ's body: "Now you are the body of Christ and individually members of it" (1 Cor 12:27 NRSV), a transition that narrows the focus to the particular shape of the local body in Corinth. This is significant, New Testament scholar James Thompson argues, for it is here we see Paul's vision for care of the weakest taking root at the local level. "The local congregation is the place for care of the most vulnerable in society," Thompson writes. "The local congregation is small enough to recognize the special needs of its members."[26] What emerges in Paul's letters to the churches, Thompson proposes, is the portrait of the apostle first and foremost as a parish pastor, his letters betraying a bias toward the local church for how ministry to those who are most in need shall occur. To more fully understand this point, it is vital to see that the passage on the body of Christ in 1 Corinthians chapter 12 is followed immediately by the famous passage on love in chapter 13. Even though we tend to hear these verses most often spoken at weddings, Gorman laments that the passage is often misunderstood and read out of the context. Those verses are meant, Gorman argues, to give specific shape to what it means to live as a member of the body of Christ. When seen in light of the vulnerable interdependence of all members of the body, then, the embodiment of love that does not insist on its own way (1 Cor 13:5), that bears all things, endures all things (1 Cor 13:7) is in fact the description of cruciform love that follows from the vision of cruciform living for members of the body of Christ.[27] And it is precisely the command to love one another in this self-sacrificial way that must be put into practice within the local community, Thompson insists.[28] In a similar vein to St. Teresa's prayer about becoming the hands and feet of Christ, interpreters of Paul should understand the importance of embodied acts of love toward the weakest members of the body and how such acts occur at the local church level.

Thompson's perspective is a valuable one—that Paul's vision of the body of Christ is focused mainly on local church communities because that is where care for those who are weakest must occur. At the same time, I encourage us not to ignore the wider notion of the body of Christ that is also at work in Paul's way of relating to local churches like the one in Corinth, one that does not always depend on face-to-face interaction, one that I am calling the *virtual* body of Christ.

Strong and Weak Ties in Paul's Virtual Body of Christ

Before directly addressing how "body of Christ" imagery in Paul's letters points not just to local church communities but also to the church in a more virtual, universal way, let us first return to the sociological discussion about social networks and their strong and weak ties from the previous chapter and how that discussion might connect with Paul's vision for the church as a social network. On the one hand, Thompson is making the point that local face-to-face communities are places where the body of Christ is able to tend most concretely and specifically to the suffering in its midst because the local community is viewed as the site where ties are the strongest. While it certainly is the case that participants in local communities know most intimately the needs of their own members, it is also interesting to note that biblical scholars who apply Mark Granovetter's work on social network ties often conclude that Paul himself actually had many more weak ties than strong ones.[29] They point both to Paul's use of coworkers like Timothy and Phoebe to bring his message to communities like the one in Corinth to offer on-the-ground guidance in Paul's absence (cf. 1 Cor 4:17; Rom 16:1-2) as well as to the factions that existed in the community and the direct challenges to Paul's authority (cf. 1 Cor 1:12-17) as evidence that the ties Paul formed "were not uniformly strong."[30] On the other hand, New Testament scholar Dennis Duling has recently proposed that while Paul certainly had a number of weak ties, there is also solid support for the perspective that Paul formed strong ties within both the local church networks as well as the network of coworkers who helped support and maintain his ministry to the churches in his care. Duling argues that Paul's initial stay for over a year in Corinth, coupled with his second (2 Cor 2:1) and possible third visits (2 Cor 12:14; 13:1), as well as his pledge to "spend some time" with the Corinthians (1 Cor 16:6-7), all suggest, in the language of networks and ties, a "social network of some duration or social interaction, one index of intimacy, thus the likelihood of 'strong ties.'"[31] Furthermore, Paul's discussions of those with whom he reportedly stayed while in Corinth— Aquila and Pricilla (Acts 18:1-3; 1 Cor 16:19), who also accompanied him from Corinth to Ephesus (Acts 18:22-3), and Gaius (1 Cor 1:14; Rom 16:23), whom Paul himself baptized—indicate he built strong ties with individuals within the Corinthian community. Intriguing new research on the makeup of these early churches suggests that churches like the one in Corinth were likely made up of people of differing wealth and social rank from society's upper echelons all the way down to slaves and ex-slaves. Thus these networks being formed by Paul and his vision of the body of Christ indicate that weak ties mingled alongside strong ties and also that this vision of a body where all members depend on all other members encouraged the formation of strong ties within Paul's expanding network of churches in the arm of the Mediterranean Sea east of Greece.[32]

While it is helpful and important to understand Paul's network as one made up of both strong and weak ties, a point often overlooked in these discussions is that Paul himself—even as he spent a year or more being physically present with churches like Corinth before moving on—is nevertheless more often a part of all of the particular local bodies of Christ in a virtual rather than a physical way. This point highlights once again the inadequacy of thinking about the term *virtual* as meaning *almost*. Paul is decidedly more than *almost* a part of these communities; he is founder, leader, guide, and inspiration to multiple church communities simultaneously. In his letter to the Philippian church, a community he founded, the strong ties he formed in the time he spent physically with them appear not only through Paul's expression of deep affection for members of the community (Phil 1:3), but also in the comfort he found in knowing that the community held him in their heart (Phil 1:7). Even as he developed many close relationships through face-to-face interactions with members of the churches scattered across the Mediterranean, it is also the case that he was only able to be physically present with them on very occasional visits. That Paul's relationships with the ancient churches are maintained primarily through the back and forth of letters has led pastor and writer Jason Byassee to propose that even in its earliest incarnations, the body of Christ has always also been a virtual body.[33] Indeed, if we return to the vision that confronted Paul on the road to Damascus, we find a Paul who heard a voice (in a virtual encounter?[34]) saying, "Saul, Saul, why are you harassing me?" (Acts 9:4). It is important to note that Paul was persecuting the followers of Jesus rather than the *person* Jesus who lived, died, and rose before Paul took up his role as a persecutor of those who followed Jesus. In other words, from the very beginning of his relationship with Jesus and his followers, Paul's connection to Christ was a virtual one, mediated primarily through his followers.

Paul describes his brothers and sisters in Corinth as members with him in Christ's body, but his presence with them is once again primarily a virtual one, mediated through letters and messages passed on by Timothy and other coworkers. In order to maintain ongoing relationships to these communities, Paul developed and relied on a network of letter coworkers, cosenders—and sometimes even cowriters—with whom he worked to get letters delivered to the churches and responses brought back to him.[35] Byassee offers this intriguing view of Paul's relationship with the church communities he leads, most often from a distance:

> Paul so often longs to be with the congregations from whom he is absent in the body. But notice what he doesn't do: he doesn't wait to offer them his words until he can be with them. He sends them letters. Letters meant to be read corporately, perhaps even to lead worship or be part of it. Such letters allow him to engage personally without being present personally. They are a poor substitute in some ways. In others they are superior.[36]

Paul's connections with all other members of local incarnations of the body of Christ are nurtured and maintained mostly through a virtual form of communication. To talk about letters as virtual communication helps make more visible the ways in which communication was also mediated during predigital periods of history.[37] And as Byassee suggests, Paul's virtual presence via letters is in some ways, for both Paul and the community, a poor substitute for his actual physical presence among them. We see from the first letter to the Corinthians, for instance, that Paul is very distressed over some members of the community's abuse of the practice of the Lord's Supper. They reportedly eat and drink to sate their own desires while others go hungry (1 Cor 11:17-22). It is likely that Paul's physical presence with them could have helped curtail such abuses much more quickly. Instead, such practices were able to continue far longer than Paul desired because he was dependent upon the slow-to-arrive letters addressing such problems. And as Paul wrote to church communities like the one in Philippi about his times in prison, he took solace in knowing of the prayers and virtual support from the community, even as he longed for the comfort of their physical presence during his imprisonment (Phil 1:8).

In other ways, though, the letter writing approach opens up new avenues for developing and maintaining important relational ties, both strong and weak. As Elizabeth Drescher observes, Paul's pastoral ministry via letters presents an innovative, decentralized model of leadership that we can learn from today. Calling Paul a "networked communicator," Drescher points out that when communication between pastor and congregation happens primarily through letters being read aloud to the community, as is done with Paul's letters (cf. 1 Thess 5:27), the community is invited not just into dialogue with Paul through the contents of the letter but also into engagement with one another over how the contents of the letter should be interpreted each within its own particular context. When we read Paul's letters to the Corinthians as well as his other letters, we see in them a pastor who offers encouragement, consolation, critique, correction, solace, instruction, and admonishment—and each of his letters is full of theological responses shaped by the on-the-ground experiences of the members of the body of Christ.[38] Following his instruction to the Corinthians on what love looks like among members of the body of Christ in 1 Corinthians 13, we see Paul in chapter 14 explaining how that same vision of cruciform love applies to judicious uses of spiritual gifts in worship.[39] It is clear that Paul's leadership and guidance through his letters shaped how these fledgling churches attempt to live into what it means to be the body of Christ; at the same time, this primarily virtual approach to leadership empowered agency and lay leadership within the communities as they put into practice this vision of community and ministry.

Returning to the question of whether ministry to the weakest members of the body happens only at the local level, we see in Paul's virtual presence, leadership, and ministry to communities at Corinth and beyond that care for all members was occurring through his letters and through the ways in which those letters shape and sometimes correct the concrete practices of these church communities. His continual attempts at resocializing members of these communities to more fully embody "God's arrangement" of the body of Christ had on-the-ground ramifications. As Drescher notes, when Paul interrogated the Corinthians with "Was Paul crucified for you, or were you baptized in Paul's name?" (1 Cor 1:13-14), he modeled an "embodied spirituality" that connected to a particular way of living in defense of the gospel that led to persecution, and he invited others to respond with similar commitment.[40] Most often from afar, Paul directed their attention toward the one who was crucified, in whose name they were baptized, in order to more fully understand the form their collective lives should take as followers of Christ.

The Virtual Body of Christ and the Church Universal

Even as Paul used body of Christ imagery in 1 Corinthians (and in Romans) with the local community in mind, there are other New Testament letters where this imagery is also linked to a more universal, cosmic view of the body of Christ. While it is the case that Paul never established a structure linking multiple churches together in any formal way and that scholars continue to debate to what extent Paul understood the body of Christ in universal terms, it is important to understand that Paul imagined the church not just in local terms but also as extending beyond the individual local communities. For instance, Paul admitted to having persecuted "God's church" in the letters to the Galatians (1:13) and Philippians (3:6) and in so doing reflected an understanding of the church as more than simply a local phenomenon. His Galatians letter is addressed to "the churches in Galatia" (Gal 1:2), suggesting not just geographical proximity but also common cause among multiple communities. In his salutation to the Corinthians, Paul addressed the letter "to God's church that is in Corinth" and also "to those who have been made holy to God in Christ Jesus, who are called to be God's people. Together with all those who call upon the name of our Lord Jesus Christ in every place—he's their Lord and ours!" (1 Cor 1:2). Further, it is probable that Paul understood traditions such as the Lord's Supper as common to all church communities, as instructions about the meal are given in Paul's original set of teachings about it (1 Cor 11:23-26) and were likely given to all communities being guided by Paul. These examples help flesh out the claim that for Paul, the local church was also always connected to a larger vision of the body of Christ.[41]

Thus far, the discussion has focused on the body of Christ imagery in what scholars refer to as the "undisputed letters" of Paul (letters such as 1 Corinthians around which there is consensus that Paul actually wrote them) and not on the imagery as it appears in "disputed letters" like Colossians and Ephesians. Despite the fact that there is debate about whether or not Paul actually wrote these letters (because they differ in wording, style, and theology from the undisputed ones), it is nevertheless worth examining what these disputed letters say about the body of Christ, as they are written in Paul's name and are included in Christian scripture. The letter to the Colossians is written to a community Paul never personally visited; still, the letter suggests that he was related to the members of the church in Colossae as "brothers and sisters in Christ" (Col 1:2). Ephesus, on the other hand, is a town where Paul is thought to have spent significant time (cf. Acts 18:18-20), but the letter to the Ephesians, it is important to note, does not reference any specific issues arising from the church in Ephesus, casting doubt on whether it was actually written to a specific church community or was instead a letter summarizing Paul's teachings that circulated more broadly. Both of these letters include wider, cosmic visions of the body of Christ, and when their visions are coupled with emphasis on the local church in Paul's other letters, we can see that Paul's vision of the body of Christ went well beyond an "insular focus of the local congregation that was concerned only for its own welfare."[42] How, then, do these additional letters enhance our understanding of Paul's vision of a virtual body of Christ?

The letter to the Colossians was written to a church community that Paul became familiar with through a Christian minister named Epaphras (Col 1:7-8; 4:12-13). A central purpose of the letter was to warn against a philosophy in vogue at the time in Colossae that, according to the letter, was leading people away from Christ (Col 2:8). While scholars continue to debate the origins of this philosophy, there is broad agreement that practices of self-abasement and extreme asceticism stand at its heart (Col 2:21, 23).[43] The letter is written to reassure the Christians in Colossae that membership in the body of Christ does not demand such severe ascetic practices. A central message of the letter is that it is God who reconciles all things (Col 1:20) rather than those who follow a particular set of stringent philosophical practices.

Discussion of the body of Christ comes in Colossians 1:15-20, a section that is in the language of an ancient hymn or poem. This passage draws on imagery from the Old Testament wisdom tradition (cf. Prov 1–9) and presents a view of the cosmic lordship of Christ as having secured reconciliation for the church, even amid all the earthly powers that threaten it (Col 1:16). The poem emphasizes that all that is has been created through Christ and is held together in him (Col 1:17). And while the image of the body of Christ in 1 Corinthians highlights the interrelationship between the members that leveled conventional understandings of social hierarchy, here Christ is depicted as the head of the body, that is, the church (Col 1:18). Even with this difference, Michael Gorman proposes that some strong commonalities exist between the vision of the body of Christ in Colossians and the vision we examined earlier in 1 Corinthians. For example, the Colossians hymn, even with its cosmic imagery, still affirms that the preexistent Christ is also the crucified Christ (Col 1:20). Once again the church community's attention is directed toward Christ's death; then there is the claim that followers of Christ have been "reconciled . . . by his physical body through death" (Col 1:22). Existence within the body of the cosmic Christ is here the source of a new humanity as well, where distinctions like "Jew or Greek, slave or free, male and female" are ultimately overcome (Col 3:28), even as, discomfortingly, the rules listed for Christian households in Colossians 3:18–4:1 advocate for wives' submission to their husbands and slaves' obedience to their masters. The household codes listed here and in Ephesians, according to feminist New Testament scholars like E. Elizabeth Johnson, lend more credence to the claim that these letters were not written by Paul. For, as Johnson points out, the Paul of the undisputed letters is not much interested in traditional hierarchical household order. From his counsel that it is better not to marry (1 Cor 7:8) to the declaration in Galatians 3:28 that distinction between male and female, slave and free are no longer operate in the body of Christ, Paul's writings often challenge such a vision for the household.[44] Even as there is cause to distance the household codes from Paul, it is also worth noting that in the Colossians version of the code, love becomes the guiding value for family life, an aspect of hierarchical ordering missing from other household codes of the time.[45] Therefore, even with the vision of what it means to be human as a member of the body of Christ offered in Colossians 1:15-20 being challenged by the hierarchical ordering of relationships in chapter 3, it is still possible to glimpse a distinctive countercultural vision for a new humanity, not just for the wider church but particularly, too, for the local church at Colossae, where the popularity of severe asceticism and self-abasement had threatened the local church.

As highlighted earlier, it is unclear whether or not the letter to the Ephesians was actually addressed to the particular church in Ephesus. Earliest versions of the letter omit the phrase "in Ephesus" from the opening greeting "to the holy and faithful people" in Ephesians 1:1. The letter does not move, as most of Paul's letters do, from general to specific; furthermore, it assumes no personal contact with Paul (Eph 1:15; 3:2) even though he spent considerable time there.[46] The letter shares much in common with the letter to the Colossians in terms of vocabulary, structure, and theology; therefore, it is not surprising that the letter to the Ephesians also shares with Colossians imagery of the body of Christ with an exalted cosmic Christ as its head (Eph 4:7, 15).

While the 1 Corinthians vision of the church as the body of Christ stresses both unity among as well as the distinctive roles of each member of the body, the emphasis in Ephesians is much more on the oneness of the body. Headed by Christ, the body "grow[s] in every way into Christ" (Eph 4:15) but is held together firmly through what are commonly referred to as the "seven unities of the church": one body, one Spirit, one hope, one Lord, one faith, one baptism, and one God (Eph 4:4-6). Ephesians returns to the same key theme from 1 Corinthians: that when all the ligaments work together, the body will be able to build itself up in love (Eph 4:16), although the letter also includes the ordering of the Christian household with men as subject to Christ, the head of the church, women as subject to men, who are head of the household, and slaves subject to their masters (Eph 5:21–6:8). Once again, it is important to point out the way in which the household code stands in stark contrast to Paul's endearing tribute to female leaders who served alongside the male ones in the church in Rome (Rom 16:1-16).[47]

A couple additional observations are worth making about the discussion of the body of Christ in Ephesians. Verses 4:1-3 make up the preface to the rehearsal of the unities of the church and include the depiction of Paul as a "prisoner for the Lord." Here the apostle's life is presented not just as a model of faithful living but the apostle himself is also understood as a member of the body of Christ—even when he is far away and in prison—who makes "an effort to preserve the unity of the Spirit with the peace that ties you together" (Eph 4:3). This passage positions Paul as belonging not just to the local body of Christ in Ephesus (remember: the image of the body of Christ in Ephesians is presented in less particular, more universal terms) but also to the *one body* as it is incarnated in Philippi and Corinth and Colossae, in Ephesus and Rome. Put another way, Paul (or the author writing as Paul) is claiming membership in the virtual body of Christ. In addition, this preface sets the fact of Paul's imprisonment alongside his plea that fellow Christians lead a life worthy of their calling as members of the body of Christ (Eph 4:1). Just as in 1 Corinthians (12:7, 11), this letter affirms that every member of the body (Eph 4:7) has been granted a spiritual gift that issues from divine grace. At the heart of each gift, we see once again, is the ability to live out the call to "[bear] one another in love" (Eph 4:2 NRSV). Unlike 1 Corinthians, though, Ephesians attributes this gift as coming specifically from Christ rather than from God or the Spirit (Eph 4:7-11; cf. 1 Cor 12:11, 18, 28), which is consistent with the stress in the letter on Christ's cosmic sovereignty. Ephesians 4:1-16 concludes with the image of the immature body growing into a maturity exhibited by the head, Christ, where such growth allows the members of the body to live out their various calling in love.[48] While this letter's imagery of the body does not explicitly discuss how members should treat the weakest members among them, the repeated admonition for members to embody their call to love all other members of the body reveals that this vision of the wider, virtual body stands in strong sympathy with the 1 Corinthians call to pay particular attention to the weakest members.

The Body of Christ Will Always Be a Virtual Body

What I have sought to show thus far in this chapter is that from its inception, Paul's radical, unconventional vision of church has not just been about local communities of faith but also about what I am calling the virtual body of Christ, a body that is wedded to but also transcends specific, individual incarnations of church. The task for the remainder of the chapter is to show that the church's vision for the body of Christ since the time of Paul has continued to include a virtual community alongside its local iterations.

The story of the growth of the church from the time of Paul to the present, it could be argued, is at once a story of the emergence of the global church representing the largest faith in the world, while also a story of communities of faith that are deeply divided and in conflict with one another. From the first century CE, churches in the East understood Christian faith and practice in increasingly divergent ways from churches in the West, eventually leading to schism in the Middle Ages. And in the Western church, significantly different visions of what it means to be church led to Protestant versions of church breaking away from Roman Catholicism, and further still, to centuries of persistent fracturing among Protestants. Even so, from the time of Paul onward, the church has also continued to turn to images like the body of Christ to indicate that somehow, someway, Christians remain linked to one another beyond the boundaries of their own local church communities or even their wider church bodies.

Indeed in the early centuries of Christianity, creeds were composed that incorporated use of the term *catholic* as a descriptor for the parameters of the church. In 381 CE, the Nicene Creed was expanded upon by a council of bishops to include the claim, "I believe in one holy catholic and apostolic church."[49] A few centuries later, the Apostles' Creed, versions of which had long been in circulation, gained its final form and, in the third article, confessed belief in "the Holy Spirit, the holy catholic church, the communion of saints . . ."[50] Even as significant numbers of modern scholars and church leaders have grown weary of the language and conceptual frameworks of the ancient creeds,[51] there are still many who likely would concur with the sentiments expressed by theologian Wolfhart Pannenberg when he observed that the creeds embody unity within Western Christianity "in spite of all the conflicts and separations" that have occurred throughout the centuries.[52] Pannenberg witnesses to the ongoing value of the creeds—not just in worship, where they express the faith of the church and connect contemporary churches to their ancient origins—but also in their potential to create common ground among different church bodies in ecumenical dialogue.[53] Critical to Pannenberg's thesis is that the creeds not only confess belief in the body of Christ in a way that transcends any and all particular iterations of the body but also that the creeds themselves continue to serve as a basis for churches that have long been separated to claim a shared history, shared foundational beliefs—and even, we might say, a shared participation in the virtual body of Christ.

The Conversion Story Continues: Embraced by the Virtual Body of Christ

Despite belonging to a church where recitation of the creeds is an integral aspect of worship, I was for many years part of that group of moderns Pannenberg referenced who have wondered (sometimes silently, sometimes aloud) about the need for continued confession of the creeds with their ancient language and concepts. Hearing church historian Jaroslav Pelikan interviewed by then *Speaking of Faith* radio host Krista Tippett on "The Need for Creeds," however, has encouraged me to acknowledge the value of continuing to recite them. Even though Pelikan, a renowned professor from Yale, could have taken a more intentionally scholarly route to explain reasons for ongoing recitation of creeds, his disarmingly personal defense of these corporate confessions of faith compels us to reconsider the creeds and what it might mean to participate in the church catholic by reciting them out loud, in worship, and together with other Christians. Here is what he said:

> My faith life, like that of every one else, fluctuates. There are ups and downs and hot spots and cold spots and boredom and *ennui* and all the rest can be there. And so I'm not asked on a Sunday morning, "As of 9:20, what do you believe?" And then you sit down with a three-by-five index card saying, "Now let's see. What do I believe today?" No, that's not what they're asking me. They're asking me, "Are you a member of a community which now, for a millennium and a half, has said, we believe in one God?"[54]

Recitation of the creeds, in Pelikan's vision, is one tangible way members of the body of Christ experience connection to that vast virtual body of Christ, one that connects us not just to other Christians around the world in the present but also to all previous incarnations of the body of Christ in the two-thousand-year history of the church.

This vision of being connected through the virtual body of Christ to past incarnations of the church has brought alive for me the power of the concept of the church universal in ways that my Protestant disposition had never before understood or appreciated. This pithy tribute to the power of our contemporary voices to join with the millions of other voices that have confessed those same words about the church catholic illuminates for me the connections I have felt when I have struggled to stand with a broken back and say those words during worship and feel the support not just of those who occupy the pew next to me but also of the love and care that comes from members of particular church communities I have been a part of earlier in my life. When I was sickest, friends from the church in which I grew up called and sent cards, flowers, and gifts. My dear friend and former coworker from the church in Baltimore where I worked after college called regularly to check in on me. People from churches where my husband and I belonged in other states during graduate school also were back in regular touch with affirmation of prayer and concern. Care from aunts, uncles, and cousins I have known all my life also made more visible for me the reality of the church catholic. A prayer shawl arrived in the mail from my aunt who is part of the prayer shawl ministry at her church in North Dakota. Flowers in the hospital and flowers at home appeared from my godmother, who was there at my baptism, and continues to pray for me daily in her farmhouse in rural Minnesota. A necklace made in honor of a parishioner with cancer at my cousin's church made its way to our home. I even received a prayer shawl from a church community in Georgia that heard of my illness, a community I have never visited and where I do not know anyone personally. And at the places of worship of family, friends, and colleagues, my name has been on prayer lists and brought forward during times of healing prayers. The examples of support coming from church communities beyond my own local community of faith could continue on for pages. It is nothing short of astounding, this awareness I have been granted, of the power of the body of Christ and its ministry to the weakest members of the body, like me. It has been humbling and moving to witness an avalanche of care that is possible only because of the church catholic that transcends the bounds of localized communities. This, again, is the stuff conversions are made of. And I want others to see what I am now able to see: a vast virtual body of Christ that began in the first century and still exists today, one that practices cruciform love to those who suffer.

While my conversion experience of being supported by the virtual body of Christ leads me to wax rhapsodic about the importance of understanding our enduring connections to members of the church in virtual terms, it is also important to be suspicious, as theologian Guillermo Hansen counsels, of any expressions of nostalgia that endorse naive views of universality and unity of the church. As we have seen, even Paul himself was not always able to fully envision and embrace all the implications of his radical proposal for the church local and universal. Yet the beauty and power of Paul's vision of the body of Christ comes in his insistence that this unity is not expressed in homogeneity but rather, as Hansen suggests, "as a network of differences that make a difference."[55] According to Hansen, Paul's recasting of what it means to be human hinges on understanding each other as simultaneously gifted as well as lacking the gifts of others, and as united with other members of the body via the mind of Christ (1 Cor 2:16). One of the great tasks before the church today, then, is to think in boundary-stretching ways about possible connections among the "swarming multitudes" that lay claim to living out the mind of Christ. Hansen suggests that whether it is the global explosion of Pentecostal churches or the multiplication of "irreverent" forms of church emerging in pubs, coffee shops, and even yurts, they are all giving expression to the "new ways in which the body of Christ is networked, loosening institutional corsets, giving room to the living God." Hansen concludes his argument about the body of Christ by asserting that

> established traditions, theologians, and institutions understandably get nervous with this, but the body of Christ is neither an institution nor a society in the strict

sense of the term. It is really the expression of a swarm without a center, for Christ is mediated by a decentered and decentering network of charismata. The network, the body, is the center.[56]

I find Hansen's framing of the Pauline image of the body of Christ helpful for thinking further about the body of Christ in virtual terms. At the same time, his notion of networks needs to be stretched even further to include digital and social media networks. For it is the case that church networks are multiplying not just in the terms he proposes but also virtually in even more radically decentered networks throughout cyberspaces. The digital revolution, then, can help the church embrace its professed commitment to "catholicity" in new ways.

Even if I have persuaded readers that the body of Christ has always been a virtual body, it may still be a significant leap to the conception of the virtual body of Christ understood digitally in terms of our current technological revolution. For growing numbers of religion scholars and leaders, the virtuality and augmentation of the current age seriously threatens the possibility of incarnational living. Virtuality might indeed be real. But are virtual spaces real enough to bear the incarnation? It is to these questions and concerns we now turn.

SMS

Chapter 3
Incarnational Living in the Digital Age

Our imitation of God in this life . . . must be an imitation of God incarnate;
our model is the Jesus, not only of Calvary, but of the workshop, the roads, the
crowds, the clamorous demands and surly oppositions, the lack of all peace and
privacy, the interruptions.

—C. S. Lewis, *The Four Loves*

While Paul's image of the church as the body of Christ has been and continues to be an animating vision for Christian identity, that concept is most fully understood when placed within the larger context of the incarnation, the belief that God entered in to our fleshy, material world through the body of a human being, Jesus. In light of this central assertion of the faith, ecological theologian Sallie McFague proclaims that "Christianity is the religion of the incarnation *par excellence*."[1] From its inception, Christianity has been a religion of the body. Christians believe that God became a very particular body in a very particular time and place and demonstrated radical care and concern for the bodies he encountered, especially the most marginalized. Scripture proclaims this God-in-the-flesh to have been born in a barn, raised by a carpenter and his wife in a rural Middle Eastern town, and dedicated to eating with those whom society cast out, to healing those who were sick. But it also is a huge part of the story that the body of the Incarnate One was brutalized and killed for proclaiming the good news of God's reign, where bodies in all their diversity will experience a new heaven and a new earth. Jesus's life and the resurrection of his crucified body, scripture testifies, are all signs that God's future is on its way to becoming our reality.

Because the biblical story is full of divine attention to the particular needs of bodies, McFague proposes that we therefore would expect Christianity to be a religion that holds bodies in high regard and treats them with deep reverence and respect.[2] Writer C. S. Lewis also gestures toward this fundamental Christian affirmation of bodies with his insistence that those who follow Jesus are called to follow the lead of the incarnate God into the messy, varied places bodies are found, attending to and caring for them as Jesus did.[3] In other words, given God's commitment to bodies, it only makes sense that members of the body of Christ are going to be known for their care of bodies, particularly the weakest ones.

The shocker is that even though Christianity is at heart an incarnational religion, great amounts of evidence suggest that those who call themselves Christians too often fail to live into the reality of reverencing and respecting bodies. Whether it is the privileging of spirit over flesh, the denigration of certain (especially darker) bodies to the realm of property, the presentation of female bodies as systematically less valuable than male ones, or the rampant disregard for non-human bodies as is evident with the growing ecological crisis, much of the history of Christianity can be read as a history of rampant *dis*respect for bodies. McFague is one voice (and body) among many who call Christians to account for this disturbing and depressing history in part by insisting that at its very foundations, the Christian claim that God became a body means that the physical world—and the bodies that make it up—are valued by God and therefore should be valued by all of us. Such proclamations are at the heart of a vision for what it means to live incarnationally in the world.

In addition to the insights of Lewis and McFague, the vision for living incarnationally put forward in these pages is also indebted to the theology of sixteenth-century reformer Martin Luther. Living as a monk devoted to the late medieval church, Luther began a protest against what he referred to as the "theology of glory" that led church leaders to want to reign with Christ.[4] Similar to the approaches of Lewis and McFague, Luther advocated for a theological focus on the implications of God becoming a body in this world, a position he referred to as a "theology of the cross." What resources does Luther's theology offer those of us who want to talk about what it means to live incarnationally in the here and now? If he were responding to Lewis's quote above, Luther would likely want us to examine our motivations for attempting to live as Jesus did. In Luther's view, it would be vital that we approach attempts at following Jesus down the streets and into the crowds of those broken open by suffering *not* as ways to try to justify ourselves before God or to prove that we are better than our spiritual ancestors (although it is tempting to try to do so). And even though he did not always practice it himself, Luther would also counsel humility over our (in)ability to be able to follow in the footsteps of Jesus. Why? Because Luther believed that sin runs deep within the human psyche. While Luther's enthusiastic view of human sinfulness is critiqued by many as overly harsh and pessimistic,[5] I find this central point of his analysis of the human condition to be disarmingly accurate: that our natural tendency is to be turned in upon ourselves, a condition that can be understood as self-absorbed and in possession of an overinflated sense of self, but it can also mean (as was the case for Luther) a relentless anxiety over whether or not we are good enough, worthy enough, or deserving of love. The take-home message of God becoming a body, for Luther, is that this human being, Jesus, was in complete alignment with God, embodying God's love in the world even unto death and, through his death and resurrection, making humanity worthy before God, something we are unable to do for ourselves. Because of what God did through Jesus, Luther believed, our relentless self-preoccupation and anxiety can be left behind for a life turned outward toward the neighbor in love.

And when we turn toward the neighbor in love—which is another way of saying "when we live incarnationally"—we often, according to Luther, are going to end up getting mired in a world of hurt, being drawn into places that resemble Golgatha, the place where Jesus was killed. This is why talking about living incarnationally necessitates talk of the cross and cruciform existence. And even as critics of Martin Luther and other theologians who talk about the tight connection between incarnational living and suffering are right to raise concerns about interpretations of this connection that seem to prescribe suffering—particularly if it comes with endorsements of abuse of power that leads to suffering—I propose that at its best, Luther's theology understands suffering *descriptively*, rather than *prescriptively*, as an inevitable consequence of incarnational living. When we follow Jesus into the crowds where our hurting neighbors reside, suffering is unavoidable. With this framing of incarnational living with insights gathered from Lewis, McFague, and Luther, it is time to turn now to potential problems and possibilities for living incarnationally in a digital age.

The Digital Age as a DisIncarnated Age?

Following Jesus into the streets, the workshops, and the crowds is often a messy, dusty, even risky prospect. While in the quote at the beginning of the chapter Lewis certainly is not proposing that beliefs about the meaning of the cross and other parts of the Jesus story are unimportant, his words nevertheless suggest that it is the deep dive into the muck of our materiality that Christians are called to do as we strive to live as Jesus did. In a similar vein, sociologist of religion James Davison Hunter argues that the God of the Bible is the God to whom "presence and place mattered decisively."[6] This is the God who talked regularly with Adam and Eve in the garden, met Moses on Mount Sinai, dwelt in the ark of the covenant that moved with the Israelites through the ancient Near East, occupied the holiest of holies in the temple in Jerusalem, and was present with Israel even in the depths of their captivity in Babylon. And for Christians, nowhere is the importance of presence and place for God more apparent than in the incarnation, God enfleshed in the person of Jesus of Nazareth. Because presence and place are so significant for this God of ancient Israel who became incarnate in Jesus, Hunter insists that presence and place should also matter acutely for all of us who worship this God. But for Hunter and a growing number of scholars of Christianity, it is precisely this issue of incarnation—of God enfleshed in the world—and incarnational living by those who follow this God that are under serious threat in the digitized age.

One aspect of digitized culture that is especially disturbing for Hunter is the way in which presence and place seem to matter much less than they once did. "We are, of course, present in time, but less and less present" because of our constant preoccupation with what is on our mobile device or our iPad, laptop, or desktop. Because of our ability to communicate with anyone at any time, Hunter laments that "presence and place simply matter less. . . . We are, in a sense, released from the gravitational pull that presence and place once necessitated for both relationship and labor."[7] Imitating Christ by following him down the road and into the crowds, Hunter argues, becomes significantly more difficult if presence and place are largely neglected in favor of virtual, dislocated connections.

The digital revolution's threat to incarnational living also plays a prominent role in Australian missiologist Michael Frost's recent book, *Incarnation: The Body of Christ in an Age of Disengagement*. In it Frost proposes that if Christians are going to live incarnationally, we first have to understand what we are up against in terms of the "excarnated nature of contemporary life."[8] The technical meaning of the term *excarnation*—also known as *defleshing*—comes from the ancient practice of removing all flesh from the bodies of those who had died, leaving only the bones. Frost utilizes this terminology to drive home his claim that "we currently find ourselves in a time in history where another kind of excarnation is occurring, an existential kind in which we are being convinced to embrace an increasingly disembodied presence in our world."[9] While Frost admits that the digital revolution does not bear sole responsibility for the current state of excarnated existence, he nevertheless is quick to blame increasing digitalization as a primary culprit. The first chapter of his book entitled *Rootless, Disengaged and Screen Addicted* takes on a variety of emerging challenges caused by current technological developments, especially people's growing attachment to their mobile devices. The 2012 Commonsense survey results Frost cites are worth quoting at some length:

> A recent study found that 41 percent of teens describe themselves as "addicted" to their phones. Forty-three percent of teens wish that they could "unplug," and more than a third wish they could go back to a time when there was no Facebook. Some teens get frustrated by how attached their friends and parents are to their own devices. For example, 28 percent of those whose parents have a mobile device say they consider their parents to be addicted to their gadgets, and 21 percent of all teens say they wish their parents spent less time with their cell phones and other devices. Nearly half (45%) of all teens say they sometimes get frustrated with their friends for texting, surfing the Internet or checking their social networking sites while they're hanging out together.[10]

Frost adds to this sobering onslaught of statistics a discussion of how ease of access to Internet pornography sites is leading to growing addictions to pornography, especially those of boys and young men. Shifting more squarely to the realm of the church, he unleashes strong critiques of church ministry done via satellite links, insisting that such forms of virtual worship not only court idolatry but are also emblematic of the ways in which contemporary excarnate Christianity separates spirit from flesh. Frost concludes his chapter with the call for Christians to embody faith and life in the company of those who have fallen "for disengagement and objectification, for screen culture and virtual reality."[11] The digital revolution, Frost proclaims, fosters a defleshed culture of disconnection where incarnational living is harder than ever before.

Both Hunter and Frost represent a sentiment common among Christian leaders and scholars who want to focus on the wide-ranging negative implications of the digital revolution, especially with respect to Christian commitment to incarnational living. For a religion that emphasizes close connections through embodied relationships, a digital age that is seen as fostering disconnection and disembodiment is particularly threatening. For a religion where presence and place matter deeply, the distractions and rootlessness purportedly fostered by digitzed living pose serious obstacles to being present in a particular time and place as Jesus was and as Christians are called to be.

While I see more possibilities in the digital revolution for incarnational living than either Frost or Hunter, it is the case that they both raise important issues that should not be ignored. Those of us attending to the potential usefulness and even advantages of digital connectivity need to be ever mindful not just of their potential for misuse but also of the ways in which the revolution is shifting cultural habits and norms in negative directions. At the same time, however, we must not neglect the fact that living incarnationally—attending to the importance of all the bodies God creates and loves—unfortunately has been a serious challenge for Christians of every age. We live in a fallen, sinful world, where preoccupation with power, prestige, and building up the self with lack of regard for others too often blinds us. Therefore, even as it is necessary to appreciate the particular challenges posed by the current digital revolution, we must also be honest and admit that Christians' inability to embody incarnational living is a very old problem. Still, highlighting Christians' perennial failed attempts should not deter us from attempting to live out our call to follow Christ down the dusty streets and into the interruptions where others are suffering and in need of care. And it is my proposal that our digital tools and virtual spaces might even offer some underappreciated potential for doing just that.

Incarnational Living beyond the Real/Virtual Divide

Even as we need to be attentive to the problems the digital revolution is helping to create or exacerbate, I want to call us back to the importance of seeing time spent online in virtual worlds as potentially more continuous with rather than always or only discontinuous with our material, embodied existence. To deepen our understanding of the close relationship between virtual and actual worlds introduced in chapter 1, I turn to theologian Kathryn Reklis's critique of the common characterizations of virtual interactions and practices as disembodied and therefore less desirable while actual interactions and practices are embodied and therefore good.[12] Reklis is a participant in the New Media Project, a group of scholars and pastors thinking together about how the digital revolution is impacting religious thought and practice. While she acknowledges ways in which attachment to digital tools cause real problems (leading, she acknowledges, to the development of "Internet rescue camps" like those in South Korea to help young men and boys break their addiction to digital life), Reklis points out that there are many embodied practices in the actual world that are neither healthy nor good, demonstrating that embodied reality cannot be uncritically lauded as good and superior to what happens virtually when our lived experience reflects a more complicated and often more continuous reality. Feeding an addiction to drugs or alcohol, for instance, frequently leads to disregard for bodily safety. Addictions and their effects are deeply embodied even as they are also psychological, mental, and spiritual. While we cannot and should not neglect cases where people are so obsessed with participation in virtual spaces that they neglect the needs of their bodies,[13] Reklis's perspective is helpful in moving the conversation beyond "seeing the real versus virtual divide in terms of embodied versus disembodied" to thinking instead "about the new permutations of digital and virtual technology informing our lives as particular ways we are embodied."[14]

In her research with churches attempting to navigate the digital revolution, Reklis has been listening to concerns voiced by church leaders about the limits of technology that have strong affinity with the concerns raised by Frost and Hunter. For instance, Reklis heard from a pastor in Seattle who resists the idea that church could be fully online because the church is "an incarnational people" that requires interaction between God and one another. Reklis notes the presumption in this statement is that real interaction must occur face-to-face rather than in online environments. The pastor is assuming a fundamental discontinuity between human interactions virtually and human interactions that take place in person. In contrast, Reklis wants to stress the continuity between virtual and actual interactions. Whether or not a particular human interaction is real or good, Reklis insists, "requires more than assessing whether it is virtually mediated or not."[15]

Without dismissing as inconsequential emerging concerns about how digital connectivity can at times create obstacles to incarnational living, Reklis affirms a point vital to my proposal about the value of the virtual body of Christ: that incarnational existence is not only possible but also might even be enhanced at times by virtual connections made online, especially when we understand those connections as more continuous than discontinuous with face-to-face ones. To explore the potential of virtual interactions to support an incarnational theology and approach to living, I return to my own conversion story of the aftermath of living with a stage IV cancer diagnosis and the healing power of virtual connections.

The Conversion Story Continues: Healing Presence in Both the Physical and Virtual Worlds

In the early days following my diagnosis of metastatic cancer, I was put on an intense regimen of radiation treatment for my fractured vertebrae, hip, and pelvis in attempts to prevent further breakdown of my bones by the disease. From the very first treatment session, I was plagued with nausea and vomiting. Given the compromised state of my spine, the heaving that accompanied my vomiting produced almost more pain in my back than I could bear. I significantly reduced what I ate, partly due to the nausea and partly out of fear that what went down would have to come up, which would translate into an exponential increase in pain. The day after Christmas in 2008, the intensity of the treatments propelled me to the point where even sips of water caused me to vomit. My ER visit the following morning led to almost a week in the hospital where additional tests determined that the radiation doses were too strong and therefore too disruptive to my intestines. The intensity of the radiation was reduced and the vomiting subsided. But I entered the new year with my body in a seriously compromised state: I had lost so much weight my ribcage showed through my skin; I needed help doing anything besides lying in bed; and I was completely undone by this radical alteration of my world.

What does incarnational living look like for someone whose body is in such a seriously compromised state? Christians are called to be present with the sick not simply to help them do the things they cannot do for themselves (make meals, do laundry, go shopping) but also to be with them when they are full of grief and despairing of their condition. I agree with theologian Stanley Hauerwas when he insists that the church is living out its calling as the hands and feet of Christ when it is "a people who have learned how to be faithful to one another by our willingness to be present, with all our vulnerabilities, to one another."[16] Hauerwas continues by suggesting that it is "our willingness to be ill and to ask for help, as well as our willingness to be present with the ill" that is a "form of Christian obligation to be present to one another in and out of pain."[17] It is vital to affirm that there is no virtual substitute for physical assistance in getting dressed, having meals provided, being given rides to and from medical appointments, and having another sit by our bedside when those of us who are ill are too sick to leave the house. I know. I have experienced all of these expressions of care firsthand. Those who have been physically there for me in those times have given me and my family gifts that could not have been given any other way.

At the same time, even as the physical presence of others offers deep comfort, it can also bring additional stress to the minds, bodies, and spirits of those who are ill. When our bodies are racked with illness, it can be very difficult to view our own embodied existence in any kind of positive light, and that makes it more difficult to interact with the bodies of others. Sociologist Arthur Frank hits the nail on the head when he writes that "during illness, people who have always *been* bodies have distinctive problems *continuing* to be bodies, particularly continuing to be the same sorts of bodies they have been."[18] Living with a serious illness, Frank continues, means learning to live with the loss of control, especially of and in one's body. And when it is one's body that is out of control, being physically present with others can be discomforting, embarrassing, even humiliating.

Frank's observations map my own experiences of being seriously ill. During the worst of my illness, I found the many losses caused by the cancer I had to negotiate were not only terrifying but also virtually impossible to talk about. Those who have been on massive doses of painkillers, for instance, know how constipation can become a virtually all-consuming concern. And when you are steeped in the anxious reality of serious constipation, being in close physical proximity to anyone who is not a medical professional only heightens the anxiety. On top of physical losses, loss of emotional stability is a constant threat for many of us who experience sudden serious illness. For several months after the diagnosis, I often would be crying before I even made it into the same room as anyone who came to visit me. Certainly crying is a natural, expected reaction to having one's life undone. And many loved ones and friends with whom I cried offered real comfort in that time. But sometimes becoming undone in the presence of one person after another not only increases the physical, mental, and even spiritual exhaustion those of us who are really sick experience, but it also can reinforce the fear (as we come face-to-face with the myriad of ways that being ill has distanced us from what it looks like to be well) that our former lives are over, never to return again.

The fear that having a well-functioning body is a thing of the past also ties into Arthur Frank's use of sociologist Erving Goffman's influential work on stigma. Goffman's point is that when we become seriously ill—especially when that illness is manifest visibly in one's body through limited mobility, loss of hair, loss of control of bodily functions, and so on—the illness imposes a stigma on the "body-self" of the one who is ill. One of the worst things about being so physically compromised (in addition to the inability to do so many of the daily tasks the able bodied take for granted) is having to witness the "seriously ill"—*dying, perhaps?*—stigma reflected back in the shock, pain, grief, and occasional pity registering on the bodies of those you encounter after becoming ill. Of course, these are all basic and understandable reactions to seeing someone we care about so changed from how we knew them to be in the (very recent) past. Even as I have witnessed that stigma in others' views of me, I also am well aware that I have had similar reactions with others in my life whose bodies have been radically altered by illness. The point here is that being embodied and being stigmatized by serious illness impacts face-to-face interactions in messy, often discomforting ways.

As we think about articulating an incarnational theology for the digital age, it is vital to make space for my and others' admittance that there are times where the reflection of our broken bodies in the eyes and bodies of others is almost too much to bear. In face-to-face encounters, we can be confronted not only with the stigma of our illness but also with an overwhelming sense of ourselves as diminished selves. Time spent in close physical proximity with others, while many times deeply comforting, at other times can also reinforce our worst fears that we really are barely hanging on, no matter how much we try and convince ourselves otherwise. So many times being physically present with those who are ill is superior to any kind of virtual presence. And yet, just as Jason Byassee notes with the Apostle Paul and his primarily virtual presence with the early churches, there are times when virtual presence actually can offer comfort that sometimes can be more elusive in face-to-face interactions.

Let me be clear: the take home message from the testimony above should *not* be that sick people all loathe their physical selves and simply want to occupy a disembodied space of virtual interaction. I am not counseling others to stay away from those who are sick and in need of support. My claim here is this: that for those of us who are really sick, there may be times when virtual interactions offer forms of care and support that are much more difficult to duplicate when we are face-to-face. To flesh this point out further, Arthur Frank's analysis again can shed some light on how those of us whose healthy, happy lives become virtually unrecognizable after the onset of serious illness. Expanding on Broyard's understanding of the diminished self, Frank explains that a diminished self is one that no longer desires itself. "Falling out of love with yourself means ceasing to consider yourself desirable to yourself: the ill person fears he [or she] is no longer worth clean teeth or new shoes."[19] In those early days in 2009, when my experience of my body was primarily and overwhelmingly one of betrayal, being able to engage in virtual interactions *alongside* the face-to-face ones played a vital role in helping me to continue striving to love myself and to continue cultivating a desire to keep on living. Online I could write in full sentences and not sound like I was dying. I could engage in virtual conversations without having to navigate the *I can't believe you're that sick* gaze. The tears I shed at the keyboard (most of the time) did not prevent me from saying what I was trying to say in an online post. What I wrote and posted online still sounded like the *me* I was familiar with, the *me* that was not wholly overcome by the stigma and diminishment caused by advanced-stage cancer. Those virtual interactions encouraged me to hold on to hope that I was not completely defined by the limitations of my very sick body. While my life would have been immeasurably diminished if I were to have only had virtual interactions during that most awful time of my illness, I was also helped in powerful, life-affirming ways through my virtual interactions with those who cared about and for me.

Now many readers may be thinking that the kind of living incarnationally that Lewis, McFague, and Luther envision entails precisely this: the entering into the space of shock and pain and grief with those whose bodies have been stigmatized by illness, just as Jesus did with ill people like the leper (Mark 1:40-45), the man with demons (Luke 8:26-39), or with the girl who had died and the woman who was bleeding (Matt 9:18-26). As stated earlier, it is most definitely the case that being physically present plays a vital role in supporting others who are at their weakest. I have been blessed by those who came and sat with and were present with me, especially during the times I was at my worst. But one of my biggest fears of getting that sick again is once again having to negotiate the reflection of my sick (and potentially dying) body in others' eyes, faces, and even entire bodies. Arthur Frank is again on point when he cites writer Anatole Broyard, who says, "It may not be dying we fear so much, but the diminished self."[20] Embodied existence within a seriously sick and seriously compromised body presents incredible daily challenges; having the seriousness of our illness confirmed by others' physical reactions to our bodies at times makes the fearful reality of a diminished self all the more real, which can be devastatingly painful even as we are grateful for the gift of physical presence with us in that awful space.

Presenting a thicker description of what living with serious illness looks like can help us acknowledge how very difficult it is to be physically present amid the losses, the stigmas, and the diminished senses of self, both for the one who is trying to offer comfort as well as for those who are in the midst of great suffering. For pain "isolates us from one another," Hauerwas observes, both for all the reasons mentioned above but also because those of us who are (more than less) well have terrible difficulty fully imagining the world of the ill.[21] No matter how good-willed we are, we simply are unable to take on another's pain as our own. The combination of these challenges leads Hauerwas to lay bare this most uncomfortable truth, that

> it is no easy matter to be with those who are ill, especially when we cannot do much for them other than simply be present. Our very helplessness too often turns to hate, both toward the one in pain and ourselves, as we despise them for reminding us of our helplessness. Only when we remember that our presence is our doing . . . can we be saved from our fevered and hopeless attempt to control others' and our own existence. Of course to believe that such presence is what we can and should do entails a belief in a presence in and beyond this world.[22]

Being with others in the midst of the awfulness brought on by illness or death, then, is where incarnational practices take on cruciform shape. Such presence resembles the self-sacrifice of the cross. If members of the body of Christ are going to embody a Pauline vision of cruciform love in being present with our sisters and brothers who are ill, we need to be honest with one another about how excruciatingly difficult it is to navigate the terrain of being present with those who are seriously diminished by disease and/or grief. In his proposal of what such ministry of presence might look like, Hauerwas turns to the biblical story of Job's massive loss of all his family, material possessions, and his health and, subsequently, of his friends' response. His friends come and sit on the ground with him for seven days, uttering not a word, "for they saw that he was in excruciating pain" (Job 2:13).[23] We could also say that Job's friends exemplify what Luther means when he talks about a cross-centered existence where members of the body of Christ understand themselves as called to be with those in pain, willing to simply *be with* those, who, like Job, endure appalling suffering.

Such embodiments of presence brim with discomfort over being in such close proximity to someone who has experienced great loss. Being so close to another's suffering provokes a fundamental sense of dis-ease over the lack of adequate words. Such presence sometimes even courts despair in light of our inability to fix or even help ease the awfulness. The image of Job's friends just being with him is a painfully beautiful vision of cruciform love. And I'm suggesting it is the case that this kind of being present in, with, and for the ill when they are at their worst can and does occur within the virtual as well as the physical realm.

Some who read my defense of virtual presence with the sick may claim that this line of thought made possible by the digital age is precisely the sort of thinking that threatens Christianity's call to incarnational living and that there is no substitute to being physically present with the weakest members of the body in their time of greatest need; they may even return to the claim that virtual support is *almost* support and conclude that it is just not an effective way to support people in their very worst times. They also may insist that to advocate for a legitimate role for virtual interactions to play is only going to promote a disincarnated existence with less of the vital care needed for the weakest among us.

While I would have wholeheartedly agreed with these claims before I got sick, I no longer can abide by any limited, one-sided view of what is actually happening virtually. Just as Kathryn Reklis asserts, we must get beyond thinking about physical embodied experiences as always superior and as standing over against disembodied experiences that happen in virtual spaces. That's simply not how our interactions with one another work with all the digital devices that now pervade our lives.

Incarnational Living Enhanced by Virtual Reality

In order to make the case about the ways in which virtual interactions can offer healing presence to those who are suffering, it becomes apparent that more attention needs to be paid to the ways digital tools are already enhancing peoples' lives in concrete, embodied ways. This is a point that is consistently overlooked by the scholars whose work focuses on shining light on all the potential threats to incarnational living that accompany the digital revolution. For instance, Frost tells a story of Palestinian-American poet Naomi Shihab Nye and her encounter with an older Palestinian woman during a layover in an airport. The older woman was distraught over her plane being delayed because she thought she would miss the important medical treatment she was scheduled to receive the next day at her destination. Frost recounts how Nye allowed the older woman to use her cell phone to call her son, who was planning to meet her at her destination. Nye then encouraged the woman to call other family members to let them know of the plane's delay. Over the course of those phone calls, Nye discovered that she and the woman had numerous friends in common. The story concludes with the older woman sharing homemade cookies with Nye and others waiting for the delayed flight. Frost concludes, "This can still happen. Even in the nowhereness of the Albuquerque airport, embodied community, generosity, laughter, culture, food, and family can burst forth like green shoots through the cracks in the concrete. But it's rare. And that's the problem."[24]

What is striking about Frost's use of this story is the way he glosses over the fact that it is Nye's *sharing her cell phone* with this distraught woman that plays a key role in this story. Without Nye offering the woman this digital tool that facilitated the critical conversations with the older woman's family, the lovely scenario of "embodied community" Frost applauds would have been much harder to come by. So while it may well be legitimate to bemoan the rarity of such connections, we also must resist ignoring the ways in which digital connections can and do enhance the kind of embodied relationships Christian visions of the incarnation promote.

Returning again to my own situation, beyond the affirmation that my body-self was not completely defined by the cancer that had spread throughout my body, the virtual world also opened up avenues for others to embody incarnational ways of living that mattered to me in material ways. That I could communicate with a growing network of family, friends, and even strangers about what it was like to go from a healthy, active, vibrant life to a life confined largely to our house and rooms at the clinic, treatment center, and hospital offered others some glimpses into the challenges I faced in a way that would not have been possible without virtual modes of communication. It took a while for me to realize how family members and friends utilized what I was saying about my condition to then find ways to offer help that made material differences in my new life with a seriously ill body. For example, when I expressed disappointment online that Christmas was coming and I was in no condition to visit a salon for a haircut, a mother of a friend of my daughter—who also happened to be a hair stylist—called to ask when she could come over and cut my hair at home. I gladly accepted this offer and reveled in the gift of styled hair to help counteract a broken back and depleted spirit. This illustration helps demonstrate the ways in which virtual interaction and embodied interaction are often continuous rather than discontinuous.

As is the case for many whose lives are rearranged by a serious diagnosis and bodily upheaval, coming to understand the diagnosis, treatment options, and prognosis (especially when powerful pain medications are also daily companions) is a messy, gradual process. One place I tried to lay out the terms of "my kind" of metastatic cancer was on CaringBridge. After radiation and oncology visits, I would post updates about what I had learned about my condition and the treatment being proposed. While it is the case that some people reading my updates would pass along some treatment recommendations that were unhelpful (which also happens in face-to-face interactions), I have also received numerous responses that have been really critical to helping me better understand and agree to treatment I was being told I would need. As I discussed earlier, the diagnosis of *metastatic* breast cancer was disorienting to all of us in my family who, given my mother's own breast cancer diagnosis and treatment, thought we knew the breast cancer drill. The drill recommended for my form of metastatic breast cancer, however, was different in virtually every way. Rather than the chemotherapy regimen that results in loss of hair, I was put on a monthly regimen of biophosphonate treatments, treatments designed for osteoporosis patients to help strengthen their bones. Because the cancer had metastasized to my bones, I was put on this osteoporosis treatment that has been found to help prevent the metastasized cancer from spreading further into the bones. My first treatment occurred when I was still incredibly weak, when the seriousness of the diagnosis was just settling in (I had finally found the statistics on the Internet that reported only 20 percent of patients with stage IV breast cancer are still alive five years after diagnosis). I was told that most people experience very few side effects from the treatment, but my first treatment left me confined to bed for several days, and every joint ached with pain. I wrote about this experience on CaringBridge, suggesting, as many do who undergo painful treatments when they're already really ill, that I wasn't sure I would continue with the treatments. A few hours after that post I received an e-mail from a fellow religion professor in another state whose husband is a physician and knows much more about my diagnosis than I did then. She explained to me what biophosphonate drugs do for metastatic cancer patients and why it was vital to give myself the greatest opportunity to keep the cancer in check so that I could count on some more living ahead of me. Amid my despair of my condition and the temptations to reject more treatment that made me feel even worse than my new normal of low-level awfulness, that message cut through my almost-complete consumption with my own pain and helped me agree to continue the treatment.

These stories highlight not just how virtual communication is sometimes less traumatic to negotiate than face-to-face interactions for people who are seriously ill but also—once again—that the often-intimate interrelatedness between virtual and actual worlds can together lead to better support and care not just for the soul and the spirit but also for the body. Furthermore, these stories demonstrate that presence and place do not necessarily matter less than they once did. Rather, they show that presence and place are being reimagined in the digital age. Others' presence with and for me in virtual spaces has helped me navigate the radically altered physical realities of my postdiagnosis life.

While being present virtually with someone who is in pain might at times be just what the person needs, I want to caution us against any interpretation of the value of virtual communication that puts forth the claim that shooting off a text is therefore a suitable substitute to an in-person visit with someone who is really sick or hurting or grieving. This is precisely the kind of avoidance skeptics worry our digital culture encourages. For instance, independent historian, writer, and digital skeptic Lilian Calles Barger proposes that "in cyberspace you can bypass dealing directly with my physical presence and communicate in a narrow and confined space."[25] Barger is right, at least partially: being in touch via text, e-mail, or online post *can* be used as a tactic to avoid being really present with those in need. I certainly have been on the receiving end of some virtual communication that felt like an attempt to substitute a few lines of text for taking the time a visit demands. And knowing that friends who live close by can come and see you but don't can magnify that sense of stigma illness places on those of us who live with it. Rather than simply crossing our fingers and hoping virtual communication is all that one who is suffering needs, especially when an in-person visit is possible, we can also use virtual communication to ask whether a visit is welcome. If we view the virtual and physical worlds as continuous with each other rather than as either/or options, this will help ensure that we do not use virtual presence as a way of bypassing the in-person kind.

Even with such risk, virtual presence can be a comfort to people in ways that physical presence almost never can. Sites like CaringBridge serve as a warehouse of hundreds—even thousands—of posts from family members, friends, coworkers, church members, and even strangers who want to express their care and concern for those going through a health crisis. Having this repository of support has proven to be a vital virtual place where several members of my family have gone on nights since my diagnosis when sleep has eluded them; it is a place my husband went every single day for years during lunch to read again the words of comfort, hope, and support that still exist on my CaringBridge website. To invoke once again the sociological language of social networks' strong and weak ties, it is important to note that healing presence can be mediated to those in pain not just through strong ties but also through weak ones. A good number of meals that came my family's way during those early months were from families we barely knew (weak ties), coordinated through websites that facilitate care for those in need of help. It has been both humbling and moving to witness how virtual communication is able to facilitate such tangible offerings of care and concern to those who suffer.

Just because these examples of presence and place are not identifiably physical and material in nature does not mean they are not real. These examples also demonstrate that incarnational living is not only possible in the digital age but can even be enhanced by virtual spaces and forms of interaction in a way that helps us pattern our lives after the Incarnate One who walked dusty streets to be present with those who suffer.

Incarnational Theology for the Digital Age

Our world is full of people suffering in mind, body, and spirit. And if, as I have argued, the new world ushered in by the digital revolution is not going anywhere soon, then Christians need to put forward an incarnational theology that not only approaches proliferating technologies with a healthy skepticism but also encompasses a willingness to imagine how they might open up new pathways for walking those dusty roads into the crowds of hurting people. Based on what we have learned thus far about the potentiality of new virtual pathways for bearing divine presence, what follows is an articulation of some of the animating principles of an incarnational theology in the digital age.

First, an incarnational theology for the current age needs to affirm that being present with others occurs virtually as well as physically. Presence to and with another, to borrow a phrase from Jewish philosopher Martin Buber, is fundamentally a relationship between an "I" and a "Thou." Real presence takes others seriously; it honors their sacredness.[26] We all know we can experience the real and profound presence of another person in a mediated, virtual way, whether that presence comes through a well-crafted letter (as Paul's presence often did for the ancient churches), a well-timed phone call, or more recently, a thoughtful e-mail, post, or text. Indeed, Christians have long understood Christ's presence among them to be simultaneously real and virtual. In Matthew 18:20, Jesus says, "Where two or three are gathered in my name, I am there among them." Not long after he says this, Jesus is no longer physically with his disciples; even so, Jesus insists that he will continue to be with them as they try to figure out what it means to follow him without his bodily presence to guide them. For centuries Christians have invoked this passage as evidence of Christ's enduring presence with them and with the church. In the Gospel of John, Jesus reassures his followers that they will not be alone after he leaves, but that God will send the Holy Spirit to be with them (14:26). Since the time of Jesus, his followers have been affirming the reality of divine presence in their lives.

Even though Christ is no longer present in physical form, Christians continue to speak of experiencing divine presence in embodied ways. Medieval Christian mystical writings, for instance, overflow with images of bodily responses to their experience of divine presence. St. Teresa, whose prayer about Christ having no body but ours is quoted in the introduction to chapter 2, describes "a feeling of the presence of God [that] would come over me unexpectedly, so that I could in no wise doubt that he was within me, or that I was wholly absorbed in him."[27] Another famous illustration of divine presence comes from Martin Luther King Jr.'s kitchen-table experience during the Montgomery bus boycott. Consumed by fear, King prayed for courage. "At that moment," King writes, "I experienced the presence of the Divine as I had never experienced God before." His fear subsided and was replaced by courage, resolve, and peace. Even after his home was bombed a few days later, King insisted that fear had left him and he was confident God was with him.[28] Attestations of divine presence continue in our present day from Pentecostal claims of bodies being taken over by the Holy Spirit to Quaker references to connecting to the "divine spark" that exists within us all to the irreverent Lutheran pastor Nadia Bolz-Weber's testimony of being slapped by the Spirit into noticing what God was up to in her life.[29] Such attestations of divine presence can be understood as referencing the virtual presence of God that makes an embodied difference. And in our digital age, virtual presence made possible through digital connectivity is simply the most recent form of the kind of mediated, virtual presence Christians have long affirmed.

It is also essential to notice the corporate nature of the claim "for where two or three are gathered in my name, I'm there with them" (Matt 18:20). When the Apostle Paul shares with the earliest Christians his vision of what it means to live incarnationally, he invokes the image of the church as the body of Christ, a profoundly communal vision for extending Christ's transformative presence into the world in physical as well as virtual form.

Second, an incarnational theology of the digital age follows in the footsteps of a Lutheran theology of the cross in its affirmation of the cruciform shape of being the hands and feet of Christ in the physical and virtual worlds. In this project's investigation of the specific contours of Paul's vision of the body of Christ, it becomes clear that members of the body are called to attend to the weakest among them with a cruciform kind of love that "puts up with all things" and "endures all things" (1 Cor 13:7). Embodying this kind of care for those whose lives have been undone by illness or other awfulness will take a variety of forms, depending on the kind of pain that is being endured. Even as we continue to affirm the vital role of physical presence in a manner similar to Job's friends who sat with him for days during the worst of his suffering, it is crucial to acknowledge that self-sacrificial ways of caring for those who suffer can be manifest virtually as well. Just because Jesus's disciples were in close physical proximity as he anguished over his impending arrest and crucifixion in the Garden of Gethsemane does not mean they provided any kind of comfort in that great hour of need (Matt 26:36-45). There are times when virtual conversations open up the possibility to go deep and allow those who are hurting to express the fears they dare not speak out loud, to be in touch at inopportune times when physical presence with the one who is hurting would be all but impossible. Because it is the case that we can be present with (most) others in our lives virtually via e-mail or text or on Facebook or Twitter more easily than we can be physically present with them, we must not discount the ways in which we can bear and endure with others in real ways through digital connection.

Social media strategist Meredith Gould is so convinced that incarnational presence is already happening virtually that she has revised St. Teresa of Avila's prayer, "Christ Has No Body" to be, "Christ Has No Online Presence but Yours":

> Christ has no online presence but yours,
> No blog, no Facebook page but yours,
> Yours are the tweets through which love touches this world,
> Yours are the posts through which the Gospel is shared.
> Yours are the updates through which hope is revealed.
> Christ has no online presence but yours,
> No blog, no Facebook page but yours.[30]

While the prayer might strike some as more playful than serious, it helps encourage further reflection on how Christ is present virtually via social media. Biblical scholar Andrew Byers, who writes on intersections between religion and media, offers a vision of incarnational presence in virtual space when he proposes that Christians adopt a "cruciform media ethic" for the time we spend online, which means staying away from embittered remarks in comment streams, self-centered posts that aim at boosting online significance, vain status updates,[31] and I would add, regulating the constant temptation to reinforce our identity as consumers through online purchases. We live in a world overflowing with suffering, and it is possible to utilize our digital tools more intentionally to be present with those who are in pain.

Yet again, however, the cruciform shape of incarnational living should not be understood as individualized experiences generated from one individual caring for another individual. Just as in the case of Job's friends, being with those whose lives are undone is bigger than any one of us can take on by ourselves. And while joining an online network that advocates for and brings help to those who are suffering has the potential to be simply "click activism," such actions can also be the first step to becoming seriously committed to helping alleviate the pain others are experiencing.

Third, incarnational theology for the digital age has the potential to more fully embody the ways in which Jesus's healing presence was not just for those in his inner circle (i.e., his strong ties) but just as much for those outside his circle (weak ties). Certainly Jesus's itinerant ministry opened him up for increased exposure to those outside his social network. But the pattern of Jesus's ministry is also one of being radically open to the suffering he encountered as he traveled from place to place. In the digital age, it simply is the case that our networks are expanding to include more of both strong and weak ties. While digital skeptics decry the expansive reach of virtual connections as making it impossible to determine who is our neighbor (and therefore more difficult to fulfill the call to love our neighbor as ourselves),[32] in the first half of the last century, African American theologian Howard Thurman was already talking about neighborliness as a nonspatial concept. In the telling of the story of the Good Samaritan, Thurman—a leader whose vision greatly influenced the work of Martin Luther King Jr.—suggests that Jesus is showing his followers how everyone is potentially a neighbor, regardless of class, race, or condition.[33] Through social media sites and other virtual connections, our networks expand and offer increased possibility to encounter those beyond our immediate circles who are in pain and need real presence and support.

Finally, an incarnational theology for the digital age will emphasize that even though it is vital to be present, to embody cruciform love, and to broaden that circle of care beyond the limits of strong ties in our lives, there is no definitive prescription for what following Jesus down the streets and into the crowds looks like in the twenty-first century (or in any other time). One of Martin Luther's important contributions to the understanding of Christian life was his insistence that living a Christian life is not about following a prescribed list of things a good Christian must do to earn God's love and get into heaven. Because salvation cannot be earned, then, Christians are free to serve neighbors in love, or in other words, to live incarnationally.

Even though there is no clear checklist that must be followed if one is attempting to live incarnationally, scripture nevertheless offers robust images of what following Jesus into the crowds might look like. Take the parable Jesus tells in Matthew 25:31-46. Scholars note that the parable is addressed to the churches of Matthew's audience, where (yet again) there is infighting and squabbling over who has higher status before God. The parable's sharp delineation over who is included in the coming reign of God, feminist biblical scholar Martina Gnadt suggests, is directed at those who seem to be ignoring Jesus's persistent message that the church's mission, internally and externally, is about the well-being of those whose lives are broken by poverty, illness, or incarceration. What the parable makes clear is that those who feed the hungry, clothe the naked, or visit the sick or those in prison do not view their actions in terms of a checklist for God's approval, for when Jesus commends them for their ministry to him, they ask, "Lord, when did we see you hungry and feed you, or thirsty and give you a drink" (Matt 25:37). They simply witness the needs of their neighbors and attempt to serve them in love.

It is also worth noting that yet again in this parable we find reference to the virtual body of Christ—"I assure you then when you have done it for one of the least of these . . . you have done it for *me*" (Matt 25:40, emphasis mine)— this time presented as Christ's embodied presence with those who bodies bear the effects of heart-wrenching need. Incarnational living in the digital age, then, translates into a radical openness within the community of the church not only to hearing the cries of our neighbors but also to imagining new ways of serving neighbors in love through both the virtual and actual worlds.

Just because it is possible to live incarnationally in the virtual age, however, does not mean it happens easily or frequently. Even though I am living proof of the healing love made possible through the virtual body of Christ, I agree with digital skeptic Michael Frost on this point: such transformative communion among people these days is all too rare. Therefore, the church has the potential to play a pivotal role in imagining and modeling what healthy and faithful engagement with digital tools looks like. Only when such tools are utilized in service of life-giving attention toward those who are weakest among us can they contribute to visions of incarnational living called for in the gospels.

Part Three

The Virtual Body of Christ in a Suffering World

SMS

Chapter 4

Attending to the Weakest Members of the Body in the Digital Age

You would do well to pay attention.

—2 Peter 1:19

The chapters of this book thus far all have been building a case for the existence of the virtual body of Christ in the digital age as well as encouraging Christians to acknowledge and embrace the capacity of this virtual body to be the hands and feet of Christ in the world, most especially on behalf of those who suffer. Previous chapters have engaged critics both inside and outside the realm of religion in order to raise awareness that the virtual body of Christ is already active in the world, digitally and otherwise, ministering to those who are hurting, helping to alleviate sorrow. Even as thoughtful critiques about the downsides of virtual connectivity have not been dismissed, thus far this project has sought to accentuate the positives of hyperconnectivity and the potential that resides in the digital revolution in hopes of contributing new ways of imagining our world and the way we relate to and care for one another.

So far, so good. But the time has come to linger over critiques longer than in previous chapters. More specifically, it is time to wrestle with the claims about the distracting nature of our digital devices. Why? Part of it may be because I work with young adults, who, according to recent studies, spend as much as twenty percent of class time on digital devices for nonclass purposes.[1] But that is by no means the whole story. As research cited in the previous chapter suggests, it is just as often teens expressing frustration over their parents' distracted behavior with digital devices than it is adults being frustrated with kids' use of and distraction by the latest technology. Nay, the most pressing reason to address digital

77

distractedness is simply because the virtual body of Christ cannot be a healing force in the world if people are not paying attention to the hurt that afflicts those who surround us virtually and actually.

Attentiveness under Threat

It is no doubt obvious by now that one of the central claims of this project is that 24/7 digital connectivity opens up avenues for becoming more attentive to others' needs. Recall theologian Kathryn Reklis's helpful pushback against characterizations of the virtual world as disembodied and inferior and the real world as embodied and therefore consistently superior. Reklis encourages us to envision the relationship between virtual and actual worlds as overlapping rather than oppositional, making it possible to enhance the giving and receiving of care and support during the toughest of times. Yet even as she reframes our assessment of technology in a more positive light, Reklis also recasts the issue of distraction in the digital age. The real problem, she proposes, is not that time spent in virtual worlds encourages a kind of disembodied existence, but rather that virtual and augmented realities more accurately lead to a profound "dissipation of attention and energy." Spending so much time connected to our digital devices is not as much about a lack of presence in the physical realm as it is about all of us being *too present to too many people* at the same time.[2]

Bingo. Reklis strikes a central nerve with this point. I imagine we all know exactly what she's talking about. But in case there's confusion, I offer one of my own recent experiences with dissipation of attention to flesh out her point: it came when I glanced at Facebook on my phone as I was waiting for an e-mail response from a colleague and saw a photo of one of my daughter's friends with her grandmother. I dashed off a cute comment about the photo (emoji, emoji) and clicked "POST." Back to e-mail: still no message from my colleague. Back to Facebook and the grandmother-granddaughter photo. Only then did I take time to read other comments posted below the photo, and thereby discovered that the reason this friend had posted the photo with her grandmother was because the grandma had just passed away. Ping. The awaited e-mail message arrived in my inbox. Meanwhile I was embarrassed and mad at myself for being so inattentive; I quickly deleted my cute comment under the photo and reposted a message of condolence before turning back to the pressing message from my colleague.

No doubt most of us have similar stories of how this dissipation of attention is seeping deeper into virtually all parts of life as we become increasingly wedded to our digital devices. We check our phones and return texts during face-to-face meetings for work, when we are out to dinner with friends, out walking, shopping, running errands, when we are at home (spending time that used to be reserved for those we love the most), and perhaps most dangerously, when we are driving. How is it that we are going to be able to be present to one another in incarnational ways when we are constantly giving in to the temptation to check just one more time for incoming texts, phone messages, or new updates on social media?

In addition, the increasingly ubiquitous presence and use of digital devices coupled with the sheer amount of information we interact with on a daily basis in this digital age presents unprecedented challenges to our ability to attend to what is most important. While it used to be that people received and were able to reflect on and integrate new information gradually, sociologist James Hunter stresses that receiving news of a bombing from halfway around the world at the same time as we receive sports updates and text messages from family members about dinner plans all conspire to mean that ultimately "all content is trivialized."[3] If as members of the body of Christ we are called to give our most focused attention to the weakest among us, how can we cultivate ways to prioritize the information and communication we take in each day?

Threats to our ability to attend to what matters are serious and pervasive. The supportive, healing presence of the virtual body of Christ simply is not possible without sustained attention to the other members of the body, particularly those who are struggling the most.

Practicing Sustained Attention in the Digital Age

How *do* we negotiate the constant barrage of information and messages that infiltrate our lives? Many of us likely have developed some self-imposed guidelines for keeping at least some of the distractions at bay. Whether we pledge to look up from our devices and into the eyes of our children and our spouse when they talk to us, or to attend a weekly yoga class, or to commit to keeping our phones out of sight while driving, we are aware of our growing distractedness and growing need to resist all the opportunities for distraction.

But if we are honest with ourselves, we know that real attention requires much more than simply resisting the lure of our digital devices. "Day by day we cope by selective inattention and forgetting," observes writer and spiritual director Marshall Jenkins.[4] Jenkins takes our lack of attention and moves it beyond simply a condition brought on by the technological revolution. He exposes inattention as a deep-seated practice that keeps us from having to deal with aspects of life that we might wish were not there (a broken relationship, a nagging health condition, an unfinished task), or dimensions of ourselves that we wish we could change. While attentiveness is a learned practice, it is also important to acknowledge that inattentiveness is, too.[5]

How, then, are we to work *against* the temptation to foster inattentiveness and *toward* practices of attention on what matters? According to *The Shallows: What the Internet Is Doing to Our Brains* author Nicholas Carr, in order to address the lack of attentiveness in society today, we also have to address technology's contribution to the problem. Carr writes,

> A series of psychological studies over the past twenty years has revealed that after spending time in a quiet rural setting, close to nature, people exhibit greater attentiveness, stronger memory, and generally improved cognition. Their brains become both calmer and sharper. The reason . . . is that when people aren't being bombarded by external stimuli, their brains can, in effect, relax.[6]

Carr is by no means the only one advocating for more time spent outside, in nature, to counteract changes brought on by recent technological developments. Studies report that US children spend 50 percent less time outdoors today than they did twenty years ago,[7] resulting in a condition journalist Richard Louv has termed *nature-deficit disorder*.[8] Louv's most recent book, *The Nature Principle: Reconnecting with Life in a Virtual Age*, addresses the challenge of technology even more directly when he asks, "What could our lives . . . be like if our days and nights were as immersed in nature as they are in technology?"[9] Louv's work is full of wise ways to get children and adults back out into the natural world, reconnecting with the rhythms of nature and cultivating the capacity for sustained attention for our surroundings and for one another.

Encouraging time outside in nature, free from the distractions of digital technology is an important and worthwhile proposal. Vacations with my own family have revolved around trips to US national parks; at the time of this writing, we have spent time in over twenty of them. After each trip we return home recharged with senses heightened to the beauty that surrounds us. In addition, both my daughters have been long-time attendees at a summer camp that prohibits electronic devices except on off-weekends. In this environment, all the campers have been able to practice living full days with one another in the woods without digital connections. My daughters attest that this does what Carr proposes time away from electronics will do: allows our brains to relax and offer significant opportunity to practice interacting without the aid of digital technology. Our girls have both expressed deep appreciation for being able to be in an environment where phones and Internet are not allowed. It has helped reassure them that being away from digital technology can and does nourish the soul. And they have been given weeks-long opportunities to practice being attentive to their peers, their counselors, and their natural surroundings, and they have come to see that as a gift.

Yet one of my daughters has also pointed out that choosing to be away from technology is a much different situation outside of the camp experience. At camp, *no one* communicates digitally. Outside of camp, *everyone* she knows communicates digitally. So while we can and should encourage time away from technology in order to cultivate attentiveness to others and their pain, we also must face the reality that not everyone is able to get away, and that an individual commitment to unplug from technology in a culture where all our networks rely on digital communication can feel like an unrealistic goal.

Once again, however, it is vital that we resist seeing recent technological innovations as simply existing in opposition to how we experience life in the material world. While taking our digital devices with us on a hike or to the park can encourage distraction from all the natural wonders we might attend to, it is increasingly possible for our devices to augment our experience of the natural world in ways that have the potential to cultivate attentiveness. Ben Klasky, head of IslandWood, a nonprofit organization that provides programs that immerse low-income children in outdoor settings, argues for just this both/and approach. "Designating the outdoors as a 'technology-free zone' detracts from our movement to get kids outside," he writes.[10] Apps for identifying trees, birds, and other wildlife or apps for a naturalist's notebook that encourage careful recordings of one's natural surroundings are just a few of the emerging tools that can be utilized to appreciate the natural world.[11] In addition, apps to guide us through yoga, meditation, centering prayer, and daily devotional readings from scripture are making their way into more people's lives every day. These centuries-old practices for cultivating attention are now accessible (for free or for a small cost) *through* digital media, offering even more evidence that our latest technological tools can and already are assisting people focus the mind and nourish the spirit. Therefore, even as many of us envision sustained attention being cultivated by those who remove themselves from mainstream daily life, writer Kathleen Norris, who has spent significant time around monastic communities, suggests that most contemplatives are not those who "contemplate holiness in isolation, reaching godlike illumination in serene silence, but those who manage to find God in a world filled with noise, the demands of other people and making a living."[12] Norris's vision for contemplation amid a world of persistent distractions helps illumine a vital point for cultivating attention in the digital age: that those distractions also are potential avenues to encountering not just divine presence but the presence of those who are hurting and in need of comfort.

Incarnational Attentiveness: Healing Presence in and through the Distractions

If Christian communities are to be the hands and feet of Christ in the actual and virtual world today, cultivating ways of attending closely to the stories and the needs of those who suffer is a major task before us. If the church's self-understanding is as the body of Christ, then it makes sense to study how Jesus paid attention to those who suffered.

While the Gospels overflow with examples of Jesus paying close attention to those in pain—and of that attentiveness having life-giving consequences—we are going to take a look at the final healing story in the Gospel of Mark, one of the stories where Jesus chooses interruption over accomplishing more quickly the task before him, and how this gift of attentiveness results in healing and a new future for the man who asks it of him. Paying close attention to one such story will give more specific shape to the kind of attentiveness Christian communities are called to embody in our participation in the virtual body of Christ.

In chapter 10 of the Gospel of Mark, Jesus is on the way to Jerusalem, making his way through the noisy, chaotic streets of Jericho. A man who is blind calls out to him saying, "Jesus, Son of David, show me mercy!" (Mark 10:47) Those surrounding Jesus try and fend off the distraction, but Jesus "[stands] still" (Mark 10:49 NRSV) and pays attention to the man's cries. The ensuing encounter between Jesus and Bartimaeus, especially Jesus's attentiveness to the needs of this man at the margins of the story, leads to a rebuke of the disciples' and the crowds' attempted protection of Jesus from unnecessary distractions as well as healing for Bartimaeus.

This final healing story in the Gospel of Mark offers a number of powerful insights as we consider the healing potential of attentiveness toward those who suffer. The story is set in Jericho just as Jesus embarks on the last leg of his journey toward Jerusalem. He has already (three times, in fact) told his disciples that he is on the way to Jerusalem where "the Son of David" will be tortured and killed. Biblical scholars stress the clarity and importance of Jesus's understanding of his mission at this point in the Mark's Gospel. And yet, even as the crowd rebukes Bartimaeus—*Why are you bothering him? Jesus has a mission to accomplish!*—Jesus allows himself to be interrupted by someone not just outside his circle of friends and followers, but someone whose disability sets him apart from the crowd and excludes him from the temple (cf. Lev 21:16-24).[13] Jesus, focused intently on the most significant mission of his life, finds time to be interrupted by a cry from one who is hurting, from one who yearns to be healed.

It is worth reflecting on how to interpret Jesus's response to interruption as we look for ways to pay better attention to what matters most in our lives. The previous chapter of this book began with the words of C. S. Lewis about how imitation of the incarnate God involves following him into the different places he ventured, including into the interruptions. In the digital age, with our smart phones carrying the potential to interrupt us incessantly, how do we discern which interruptions are ones that [should] matter and which ones are merely distractions?

In Jesus's case, it is important to note that he does not follow the advice of the crowd on whether or not Bartimaeus is worthy of attention. The crowd quickly determines that the blind man's need is not important enough to garner the attention of Jesus. Many in the crowd also take it upon themselves to try and silence his cries. But Jesus refuses to abide by the prevailing sentiment about what and who is attention-worthy and instead responds to Bartimaeus, and his response changes the man's life. So what is it about the interruption from Bartimaeus that causes Jesus to stand still and pay attention?

Biblical scholars point out that the vast majority of the healing stories in the Gospels depict those who are ill, or those who are friends of the ones who are ill, getting Jesus's attention.[14] In other words, Bartimaeus initiates the interaction with Jesus by crying out in pain. Only then does Jesus hear him and respond. This could lead to the conclusion that this narrative pattern of the

Gospels indicates that it is up to those in pain to let their suffering be known to others. But biblical scholar Frederick Gaiser offers a different reading of that pattern. According to Gaiser, Bartimaeus's cry is—as the cries of so many who suffer are—at base an expression of his pain, his sorrow, his anguish. To further this point, Gaiser suggests that the cries of people like Bartimaeus throughout the biblical text correspond to the structure of lament psalms—"How long will I be left to my own wits, agony filling my heart?" (Ps 13:2)—as well as to the structure of human experience. It simply is the case that people in pain "need to cry out for help."[15] But in order for those in pain to receive the help they need, someone first must hear their cry and respond. Jesus, the Gospels tell us, makes a habit of heeding those cries, even when they interrupt what many see as more pressing commitments.

In this story Jesus understands that interruptions are very often worthy of our attention, especially when they come from those who are hurting. Catholic priest and writer Henri Nouwen tells a story about a teacher who experienced years of frustration over feeling constantly interrupted by her young students, which left her feeling upset that she got so little done during her time in the classroom. Only after many years of teaching, the teacher admitted, did she discover that her interruptions "were her work."[16] Thinking about Jesus's relationship to the interruption of Bartimaeus in light of this story from Nouwen can help us recognize that paying attention to what matters most may initially come in the form of a distraction but that, with practice, we can learn to hear the laments that rise up from Facebook, Twitter, CaringBridge, or from face-to-face conversations, all crucial first steps in being able to care for those in need.

While it is important to notice both that Bartimaeus's cry initiates his encounter with Jesus and that Jesus pays close attention to the interruption that the crowd views as distracting him from his real work, it is also worth noting that some of the bystanders are converted to playing critical roles in bringing Bartimaeus to the place where healing becomes possible for him. After Jesus stops to listen to Bartimaeus's cry, he instructs others to call the man closer. Jesus's instructions affect the mood of the crowd, for some people in the crowd tell Bartimaeus, "Be encouraged! Get up! He's calling you" (Mark 10:49). Even though Bartimaeus's cry sets the rest of the scene in motion, Jesus's attention to his lament makes his suffering something of which the whole community becomes aware and prompts members of the crowd to step up and help. It is possible to imagine some in the crowd offering a hand to assist Bartimaeus in standing up, while others step back and quiet down to make room for him to move closer to the one who hears his cry. Jesus's public act of compassion ignites a change in the sentiment of the crowd, and they come to regard Bartimaeus as a person worthy of assistance and attention, not just from Jesus but from them all.

While the previous paragraphs have focused more on the actions than the specific words of the characters in the scene, the words spoken are significant as well. When Bartimaeus calls out, hoping to get Jesus's attention, his first address to Jesus is, "Son of David, show me mercy!" (Mark 10:46). To interpret his call more fully, biblical scholars point out that the Gospel of Mark operates on a symbolic as well as a literal level. In this call to Jesus, then, Bartimaeus's words suggest that the one who is blind sees Jesus for who he really is in a story where those closest to him fail to understand his identity.[17] Bartimaeus knows Jesus is a healer and calls him to attend to his needs. And as mentioned above, Jesus's recognition of Bartimaeus's suffering allows others to see his suffering as well.

It is also interesting to note that while in many healing stories in the Gospels, healing comes through touch—either Jesus's touching the one who is ill, dying, or dead, or those who are ill (like the hemorrhaging woman in Mark chapter 5) touching Jesus; in this story, Bartimaeus is healed without either word or touch.[18] As Gaiser explains, touch "is about not only physical contact but also, and perhaps more profoundly, personal interaction, emotional sharing, and mutual understanding. . . . That deeper sense of 'touch' involving words, communication, sharing, and insight" is an important element in Mark's other healing stories as well.[19] This is not to discount the ways healing comes through physical touch. At the same time, this discussion of bodily healing that comes through nonphysical means and with—or even without—words resonates with claims from the previous chapter that we unnecessarily narrow and limit the scope of healing when we limit it to being dependent solely on physical presence or physical touch. Healing presence can—and often does—manifest itself in more-than-material form.

While Bartimaeus's sight is restored without words from Jesus declaring it to be so, we should not neglect the words Jesus does use when he meets Bartimaeus face to face. Rather than springing immediately to action, Jesus asks, "What do you want me to do for you?" (Mark 10:51), opening up space for Bartimaeus to say what it is he really needs. Even though Jesus is an experienced healer, he does not approach Bartimaeus from the standpoint of already knowing what he needs. Instead, Jesus hears his cry and stops. He pauses what he's doing and then asks Bartimaeus to put in his own words what he needs most. The fact that his disability led to his alienation from the community was likely traumatic for Bartimaeus, and as trauma theorist Cathy Caruth helps us understand, those who experience trauma are in desperate need of others who understand the nature of their suffering "without eliminating the force and truth of the reality."[20] Therefore, sustained attention to the needs (spoken and unspoken) of those who live with trauma is a necessary precondition to healing.

In response to Jesus's question, Bartimaeus responds, "Teacher, I want to see" (Mark 10:51). Amid the din of the crowd, Jesus halts his entourage and gives Bartimaeus his undivided attention. Once Jesus hears that it is sight that Bartimaeus desires (v. 51), Jesus responds with, "Go, your faith has healed you" (v. 52). The story concludes with Bartimaeus regaining his sight and following Jesus on the way.

Jesus's claim, "your faith has healed you" (a formula present in a number of other stories of healing in the Gospels[21]), begs for further interpretation, as it can suggest that healing comes only if we have enough faith, and of course, many of us undoubtedly know of very devout people who have needed healing that has not seemed to come. Scholars point out that by this time in Mark's Gospel, Peter has identified Jesus as the Messiah (8:29), and Jesus has foretold his death and resurrection three times in two chapters. In other words, Mark wants hearers to understand that the reality of God's reign has begun.[22] God's reign is another way of talking about "salvation," and in the Gospel stories, health and salvation are very closely connected. In this new age of God's reign, Mark wants us to see that God is doing a new thing, ushering in wholeness and health and salvation.

But here is where the very last part of the passage becomes relevant as well: Bartimaeus, with his vision restored, gets up and follows Jesus. And where is Jesus headed? To Jerusalem, and soon thereafter, to the cross. In Mark, the first time Jesus foretells his death and resurrection (8:31), he follows it up with the proclamation that those who want to be his followers "must say no to themselves, take up their cross, and follow [him]" (8:34). When we read the story of the blind Bartimaeus in this context, we come to understand that healing is not isolated from the cross.[23] Set in the wider context of the Bible, the healing of blind Bartimaeus demonstrates that healing in scripture is understood more broadly than physical healing alone; Bartimaeus regains his sight and becomes part of the crowd following Jesus, which suggests his restoration as a member of the community. Even as he is restored as part of the wider community, the symbolism of his joining the walk toward Jerusalem and toward Jesus's crucifixion suggests that participation in the community that follows Jesus opens up those who have been healed to the suffering of others, namely, at this point, to the suffering of Jesus.

Healing as depicted in this story and many other places in scripture, then, takes on a cruciform shape.[24]

This story of healing in Mark chapter 10 has much to offer as we consider what attentiveness looks like in an age of perpetual distraction. From the cry of Bartimaeus to Jesus's willingness to pause and be interrupted to the crowd's reappraisal of Bartimaeus after taking their cues from Jesus, the healing of Bartimaeus's blindness and his restoration of community makes it possible for him to journey with Jesus and the others toward Jerusalem. Even as we take counsel from its many layers of meaning, questions remain about how stories of Jesus's healing of those who are ill relate to all who are ill today. In his work on healing and the Bible, Gaiser distinguishes between *diseases* that may be *cured* (or not) through medical means and *illnesses* that may be *healed* in emotional and spiritual ways.[25] This distinction, Gaiser is clear, should not lead to any nostalgic view of healing that downplays the value of modern medicine and the importance of increases in medical cures for illness. Instead, he proposes that Christ's healing presence with those who suffer should be interpreted within a holistic view of health that involves not just physical but emotional and spiritual dimensions as well. Gaiser proposes that, for Christians, the understanding of being well that comes from stories like the healing of Bartimaeus are "quite profoundly at odds with the world's penchant for an idolatrous understanding of health and of self." The cruciform logic at the heart of the gospel lies at the heart of these healing stories as well: it is in giving that we receive, in losing our life that we find it. "For this is not one message of Jesus among many, a hint for troubled times, a counsel of good advice," Gaiser writes, "this is the gospel itself: to lose your life is to find it. . . . It is promise, not command. . . . No bargain here, simply truth: in the giving is the finding. Not in order to, but just because it is."[26]

The story of Bartimaeus's healing also demonstrates another vital truth that must shape how we understand the Christian life as always also being a communal life:

> *We* are well, not just I. Not just the observations that one's own religious faith and positive attitude are the greatest of all placebos: "Make use of this, and *you* will feel better." But what of the other? What of the world? What of creation itself? Are they better? If those are my concerns, then the character of God and the content of faith will make all the difference.[27]

Patterns found within biblical stories of healing help make clear the corporate nature of both illness and health. Those of us who make up the body of Christ are called to embody Jesus's healing presence, as Gaiser proclaims, not just for others' well-being but also for our own. In a world where many find themselves succumbing to distractions that take them away from caring for the well-being of the whole, the church is poised to play a significant role in cultivating patterns of attentiveness to those who suffer, whether they be among our intimate relations or our weakest ties.

The Church as Countercultural Community: Cultivating Attentiveness to Those Who Need It Most

In turning specifically to the church's role in cultivating attentiveness to the needs of those among us who are in pain, I want to return to Jason Byassee's proposal mentioned in chapter 1 about possible Christian approaches to our current multifaceted technological revolution. Recall that Byassee suggests Christians neither baptize the digital revolution nor reject it. Instead, he counsels that just as with other aspects of culture, Christians need to carefully discern where and how digital communication and virtual spaces might enhance our ability to be the body of Christ in the world.

It is well known that North American churches are experiencing precipitous declines in the number of people who participate regularly in communal religious practices or affiliate with institutions called "church."[28] This continuing decline makes the defense of certain aspects of weekly worship by popular atheist writer Alain de Botton all the more intriguing. In his recent book *Religion for Atheists*, de Botton makes the [secular] case for why—even if one is disinclined to believe in God—practices like weekly worship still have value in cultures like the United States and Northern Europe, where lack of religious affiliation continues to rise. Even though he sees no need to gather in worship of God, de Botton nevertheless worries about excessive preoccupation with the individualized self in twenty-first-century societies and points to religious practices like confession—where we admit out loud our self-absorption—and weekly gathering for worship—where everyone is strongly encouraged to be introspective while also becoming more aware of others in one's own community—to be worthwhile countercultural endeavors.[29] In other words, de Botton proposes that regardless of one's theology (or lack thereof), taking stock of our inattentiveness to the world around us is a good human practice. Even more recently, de Botton has announced plans for building churches for atheists in the UK, aiming to offer opportunities for those outside religious organizations to participate in some of these countercultural rituals religions have long been practicing.[30]

For those of us who believe in God, de Botton's assessment of the value of weekly worship rituals is at best half right. For Christians, the central act of worship is praise and thanks to God, who creates, redeems, and sustains us. At the same time, de Botton's analysis of the value of religious rituals offers us some potentially important insight into the distinctiveness of religion in offering practices that cultivate attentiveness beyond one's self, especially in cultures where attentiveness to the self takes center stage.[31] This is an insight that can help support a robust case for churches playing a distinctive and vital role in guiding people toward being the body of Christ in a distracted world.

Before we get caught up in enthusiasm over the church's distinctive role in guiding people to cultivating attention, however, we must not ignore the proliferation of organizations and centers offering practices that center, calm, and focus the mind, body, and spirit. Such practices are increasingly popular not just for those who consider themselves nonreligious but also for people who understand themselves to be spiritual or even actively religious. In her award-winning book *Encountering God*, written in the 1990s, religion scholar Diana Eck writes about the growing interest (magnified significantly today) in practices that cultivate attentiveness, especially ones that originate in the traditions of Buddhism and Hinduism. Eck notes that informal "Dharma talks" about how to walk in the path of the Buddha offered at meditation centers near her home "are packed," while on any given Tuesday evening, "there is no church among the dozen in Harvard Square [near where Eck resides] that is packed with seekers who want to deepen their life of prayer; no church even opens its door for such an offering. Those who are serious about spiritual practice go to the Buddhists."[32] Eck suggests that most people frequenting the meditation centers in Boston in the early 1990s were not seeking the religion of Buddhism as much as a disciplined practice to calm and focus the mind. In contemporary North American communities, weekday practices of yoga are even more popular than the meditation practices. While Eck points out that the Christian tradition is home to many different kinds of contemplative practices—from the spiritual exercises of Saint Ignatius to the practice of *lectio divina* (reciting passages from scripture in a meditative way)—the reality [still] is that "on a Tuesday night . . . there are no introductory courses for these matters for all those [who] don't know where to begin but who are yearning for stillness of mind and heart before God."[33] What Eck observed over two decades ago is even more visible today: yoga studios and meditation centers offering hands-on guidance every day of the week on how to cultivate these spiritual practices that help increasing numbers of people—Christians among them—increase their ability to be attentive. Eck expresses concern over churches' lack of offerings to help contemporary people cultivate such spiritual disciplines. Indeed, one need only to review the growing list of books about the burnout of pastors to surmise that not enough Christian communities are cultivating spiritual practices that attend to self and others, and it affects our collective health and well being.[34]

I suggest two ways of responding to Eck's critique of North American churches: first, churches should be unapologetically clear about how weekly practices of communal worship nurture precisely the countercultural practice of sustained attention toward the weakest among us that is called for in the gospel and desperately needed in the world; and second, churches need to become more creative about presenting themselves as part of the virtual body of Christ that encourages and cultivates attentiveness through actual events throughout the week (including Tuesdays) as well as through their virtual online presence.

First, why is weekly communal worship a vital practice for Christians? While a comprehensive defense of worship is a project for another day, I want to highlight several ways in which weekly worship helps cultivate just the kind of attention that is desperately needed in our distracted culture: communal participation in the liturgy, the cruciform shape of word and sacrament, and the potential for boundary-crossing relationships forged through participation in the body of Christ.

Even though Christian worship is not unique among religious practices in its emphasis on attentiveness, it is nevertheless distinctive in its cultivation of attention not just for its own sake, not just for the practitioner's individual well being but, as Frederick Gaiser points out in the quote above, also for the well being of the entire community, especially those in need of extra care, attention, love, and support. The term *liturgy* is often translated as "the work of the people" and, as Michael Frost suggests, translates as the collective practices and rituals undertaken by the people of God that unite the community to God and one another.[35] Weekly rituals of confession of sin help us attend to our individual and collective brokenness. At the same time, the practice of weekly liturgy ushers the community through the offering of forgiveness, both in the pastor's offering of absolution for our confession as well as the movement from judgment to forgiveness in the communion meal. Through the liturgy, the congregation receives not only the promise of new life but also a new community in which to begin living out those promises.[36]

Even more, gathering together for worship offers guidance in and regular opportunities for deepening spiritual practices of prayer, meditation on scripture, and increased awareness of the needs of others. There is a rhythm to the liturgical year, beginning in the hopeful stillness of Advent, moving into the penitential period of Lent and then to the celebration of the season of Easter, and finally an entrance into Ordinary Time until we begin again with Advent. Pastor and writer Wayne Muller observes that we often think of practice—even spiritual practice— as something we should strive to perfect. But participation in the liturgical year serves a different purpose. According to Muller,

> Liturgical ritual is meant to be repeated. We are not supposed to do it right the first time and then be done with it. . . . This is not about progress, it is about circles, cycles, and the way times moves, and the things we must remember, because with ever-faster turnings of the wheel it can become easier to forget.[37]

Being shaped by these liturgical practices is a life-long process. And cultivating a spiritual attentiveness takes time. Simone Weil, a French intellectual moved by the gospel to radical action during World War II, insisted on praying the Lord's Prayer with what she called "complete attention." This prayer that Jesus taught calls forth the reign of God in the world, petitions the Lord for enough bread for all as well as for deliverance from temptation and evil. It provides a radical vision for life abundant, of life as God intends. Indeed, Weil proposes that "it is impossible to say [the prayer] once through, giving the fullest possible attention to each word, without a change, infinitesimal but real, taking place in the soul."[38] Weil's insight shines light on the ways in which prayers, creeds, and confessions often are recited with very little attention. Cultivating full attention toward each word of this prayer that envisions a new way of being in the world is a radical act, one that takes the encouragement and accountability of the whole community.

At the center of the liturgy is word and sacrament. Christians are encouraged to immerse themselves in scripture as a personal practice, but hearing biblical passages read aloud and interpreted within the community through the practice of preaching is a vital way in which Christians are shaped by those scriptural stories, such as the one discussed above from Mark chapter 10. A community shaped by the patterns of the gospel stories like the one of Bartimaeus's healing attempts to form a community "re-socialized into a way of life that posits the gospel as an alternative narrative to late modernity."[39] But such resocialization is not simply a tidy process of progress in coming to fully embody this new community. Reformer Martin Luther's view of scripture as law and gospel can be helpful in clarifying why: while Christians often mistakenly characterize the Old Testament as law and the New Testament as gospel, Luther argued for Christians to understand their relationship to scripture as a dynamic one in which the same passage will address us one day as law and another day as gospel.[40] Law, according to Luther, is that which judges and convicts, while gospel is the good news that saves. When we hear the story of the healing of Bartimaeus from a position of being sick or cast out, for instance, this story will likely address us as gospel. On the other hand, there may be times when we hear the story from Mark chapter 10 and find ourselves among the crowd who tries to silence Bartimaeus's cries for help and healing. In that case, scripture will address us as law, as judgment on our inattention to the cries of one who suffers and who is in need of attention, support, and healing.

The sacrament of communion is the place in the liturgy where the cruciform shape of Christian life is seen most clearly and vividly. The eucharistic ritual re-enacts the movement in Jesus's life from death to resurrection and links it not just to our individual and collective participation in those aspects of life that bring death but also to the vision of life in the reign of God inaugurated in Jesus. In my own Lutheran tradition, the confession of Christ's real presence in the bread and wine enacts the movement from judgment of our sinfulness to justification despite our sinfulness. The presence of Christ in the wine and bread unites us with Christ's suffering and death. At the same time, this memory of Jesus is "dangerous and subversive," as theologian Johannes Baptist Metz has argued.[41] Our union with Jesus's subversive story through communion is not just gospel for us; it is also law. Union with Christ is also judgment for the ways we participate in the suffering of others each and every day. The Eucharist—indeed the full scope of the liturgy—makes it possible for the community of sinners to be remade by a grace that permits us to forever start anew. Participation in the eucharistic meal offers the gift of starting again with the practice of being attentive to the needs within our community and to those beyond its bounds.

The practice of worship, where Christians are shaped by the liturgical rhythms as well as by the cruciform dimensions of word and sacrament, is a thoroughly communal endeavor. From the time of ancient Christianity, the Apostle Paul's invocation of the image of the followers of Jesus as the body of Christ has provided Christian communities with the framework for what it means to live incarnationally as followers of Jesus. Being part of the body of Christ means that we are called to attend to the weakest members of the body, but that call is always understood as a corporate call. Each member has a distinctive role to play in the body, and the practice of communal worship helps engender ways of thinking, feeling, and living that focus not primarily on our own needs but on those who need our attention the most.

Invoking the image of the body of Christ also helps us acknowledge not just the local church community but also the community that extends far beyond its boundaries. Martin Luther King Jr.'s famous line that Sunday mornings are the most segregated time of the week in the United States still rings uncomfortably true; even though there has been movement toward more diverse communities of faith in recent decades, local churches too often tend to be comprised of people with similar racial, ethnic, and socioeconomic backgrounds. This is another dimension of being the body of Christ where the church is called to a counter-cultural identity that does not simply mirror the boundaries often observed in the broader society. How do we go about challenging those boundaries that often constrict local churches from more fully embodying Christ's diverse body? Theologian Serene Jones proposes envisioning the church as a place of "bounded openness," where the physical and theological boundaries of particular ecclesial communities are continually

> undone by the word of God that breaks in upon it. This community, therefore, does not possess itself but always receives itself from God. This community does not own the terms by which it is collected, named, and defined; these too it receives. This community's core identity cannot therefore be defined by kinship ties, geographic region, and ethnicity. . . . Thus, at the most fundamental level, this church knows itself to be constituted by its intrinsic openness to God."[42]

Just as it was for the Apostle Paul, so it is for Christian communities of the twenty-first century: the local church continues to be a vital incarnation of what it means to be the body of Christ. And yet, the body of Christ is also called to be attentive to God's wider sense of boundedness and offer up its physical and spiritual spaces for more collective exploration of what it means to live incarnationally in the world today.

Discussing ways in which Christians are called to move beyond their own particular communities of faith leads back to the creedal confession of the church catholic discussed in chapter 2. From the time of Paul, talk of the church as the body of Christ has pushed far beyond the boundaries of the local to a claim of universality. To think more concretely about what the church catholic might look like today, theologian Cheryl Peterson suggests we think of the attribute *catholic* in a qualitative as well as quantitative way. Peterson proposes that we think of the church catholic as a community that allows itself to be "blown by the Spirit beyond the limits of particularity in order to embrace the world in all its rich diversity."[43] Our understanding of the body, then, is not simply defined by local parameters, but also by global ones, an understanding that calls us to be attentive to the suffering of those who are half a globe away. Similarly, theologian Daniel Migliore challenges Christian communities to see the call to be Christ's body as seeking a heterogeneous and inclusive community, which requires cultivation of our attention toward "strangers, people commonly considered undesirables, and even those labeled enemies."[44] This catholic sensibility can be embodied within particular local communities, whether through partnerships between congregations with divergent demographics or through work with advocacy organizations that bring faith communities together to work on issues of common concern, such as immigration rights or better resources for those struggling with mental illness. This kind of cooperation among the church catholic helps embody the call to attend to those who need it most.

Finally, it is vital that this vision of worship as cultivating the capacity for attentiveness that reaches beyond just local incarnations of the body of Christ also moves us to consider the potential of the virtual body of Christ accessible through digital communication to enhance all of the above. Even with evidence of decreased attendance at weekly worship—and therefore often decreased opportunities for the body of Christ to be formed to cultivate deep attention toward one another and the world—there is simultaneously rapid growth of churches reaching beyond their own physical boundaries through virtual spaces, particularly through live-streaming their worship services. While it is the case that most church staffs are insistent that online worship can augment—but not replace—in-person communal worship as people's means of spiritual growth or religious experience,[45] increasing numbers of church leaders are realizing the potential of online worship for helping churches embody "bounded openness" in ways that were not possible before digital technology. With online worship, communities of faith reach not just their own members but also those well beyond conventional boundaries of church.

Even as virtual worship opportunities continue to proliferate, the practice of live streaming worship definitely has its detractors. Evergreen Community Church Pastor Bob Hyatt says, "Online church is close enough to the real thing to be dangerous."[46] One of Hyatt's major worries is that people will stay home and watch a worship service on their computer and mistakenly conclude that the hour in front of a screen is what it means to participate fully in the body of Christ.[47] This is a potential consequence of having the option of online worship—that people will view in-person worship as just another distraction on an otherwise relaxing Sunday morning, thus threatening the vital communal nature not just of worship but also of the understanding that being a Christian is participation in and deep attention to the needs of the body of Christ.

But to focus narrowly on the potential liabilities ignores many other possible benefits of online worship. Stating unequivocally that online worship is an inadequate form of worship can add insult to injury for those who worship virtually because they are unable to get to church, even though they might really want to be there physically. For those who are seriously ill, or unable to get around easily due to age or disability, or weighed down too heavily by grief or depression to get to church, having the ability to participate virtually with their own church community can provide a vital link to that community in the midst of so much other loss. Reports about online worship reference young adults who stay connected to their home congregations while they are away at college, as well as church members who travel often for work being able to remain connected even when they have to be out of town.[48] And some churches that live-stream their services address the issue of potential disconnection from the wider community gathered for worship through making it possible to submit prayer requests online during worship and exchange sermon notes with others connected online. As one young man from Norway who worships virtually with a congregation from Oklahoma attests, "Technology allows us to have fellowship across borders and cultures."[49] Once again, digital connectivity has the potential to help us better be the body of Christ, both in its local and catholic incarnations.

This discussion of live-streaming worship begs the question of whether or not fully online church is a worthwhile endeavor. While I am committed to virtual practices of church augmenting rather than replacing in-person practices, compelling cases for fully virtual incarnations of church are emerging. Take the example of Extravagance, an online church community of the United Church of Christ that began and continues with a fully online format.[50] Pastor Jo Hudson testifies to the strong-tie environment that has been created with Extravagance. She "sees surprising honesty on social media. In the midst of the give-and-take of needing, caring, lamenting and hearing one another, bonds begin to form. People recognize names and hear each other's stories."[51] As mentioned earlier, fully online church goes too far for many church leaders, but if we are willing to think beyond an either/or to a both/and framework, there are certainly times and spaces where fully online churches may in fact be a vital option.

While the technological revolution is bringing with it real potential advantages to caring for those who really need help, the revolution also heightens the possibility for increased inattention to those same needs. Incarnational living calls for the cultivation of attentiveness that is attuned to the distractions that matter. In a world with increasing opportunities for interruptions, churches are primed to play a vital role in forming cruciform sensibilities of how to live with technology in ways that deepen our participation in the body of Christ. And as the church plays this role, it helps form communities that offer glimpses of that new community where all are welcome, nourished, and cared for, especially those whose lives bear the marks of deep suffering.

Chapter 5
Beyond Digital Strategies

*Becoming More Fully the Body of Christ in and
through Virtual Reality*

> *In a world that's ever changing, you, O God, are constant still.*
> *Help us in each age and season, your high purpose to fulfill:*
> *dare us to embrace new boundaries, grounded in your liberty;*
> *teach us how to be good neighbors, building true community.*
>
> *Let us be a mindful people, walking in the way of Christ;*
> *keep us from the base and shallow of a merely virtual life.*
> *Meet us in our work and worship, at the table, with our friends;*
> *usher us to life abundant with your love that never ends.*

—Ann Bell Worley, "Full of Love and Christian Virtue"

The digital revolution is changing the world in which we live, how we interact with one another, and the wider world in startlingly significant ways. Hymn writer Ann Bell Worley's lyrics witness to a hope that Christians will continue to live out the gospel in this new context. In many ways, living incarnationally amid changing contexts has always been the church's mission. As Christians seek to discern what it means to be the church during this time of technological revolution, I have proposed that the Apostle Paul's innovative imagining of the church as the body of Christ continues to be useful in framing discussions of what it means to be the church in the twenty-first century. Paul's substantial application of the metaphor of the body of Christ to the church in 1 Corinthians presents a particularly provocative image of radical interdependence among the members of the community of faith. This ancient metaphor suggests that the church, in the words of theologian Guillermo Hansen, "is neither an institution nor a society in the strict sense."[1] In a world that is being rearranged by technology, this organic understanding of church holds possibility for creative imaginings of what it means to be the body of Christ virtually and materially.

When thinking about how Paul's use of the body metaphor helps imagine what it means to be church in the digital age, religion and technology scholar Elizabeth Drescher insists that Christians can learn from Paul to "communicate, lead, and encourage [by making] use of the most relevant formats of engagement."[2] Coupled with Paul's collaborative approach to leadership (through his reliance on dozens of coworkers and even some cowriters), there is much for contemporary communities of faith to learn when contemplating their relationship to digital media. In fleshing out her point, Drescher writes,

> Paul understood that the radically transformative power of the Gospel was so significant that he couldn't rely on a narrow view of the conventions of the existing media or the long-held hierarchies of communication. In a worldview premised on the radical idea that [all are one in Christ Jesus, Gal. 3.28], Paul had a keen appreciation of the fact that his strongest voice was everyone's voice, his most authoritative words were those that encouraged everyone into community and conversation.[3]

In this age of Digital Reformation (as Drescher refers to it), the church once again has the possibility to rethink its systems, structures, and modes of communication. And because the church is an imperfect body always in need of reform, it is possible to view the massive changes being ushered in to our society via the digital revolution as opportunities to reimagine how we can better be the church in this new age.

Virtual Body of Christ Already Reforming the Church

Increasing numbers of churches recognize that certain aspects of the digital revolution are inevitable and are getting on board with producing engaging websites, creating Twitter handles, and thinking through how technology might serve the congregation's strategic vision. Digital strategies definitely have claimed a place in twenty-first-century ministry. At the same time, author of *Ministry in a Digital Age* David T. Bourgeois argues for thinking beyond digital strategies; while important for communicating information, websites only rarely convey or offer access to the heartbeat of the congregation.[4] According to Bourgeois, we live in a postwebsite world and the church's incorporation of technology to serve its mission needs to reflect that reality. This point only helps strengthen my proposal that the time is ripe to reimagine what it means to be the body of Christ in a digital age. While previous chapters have laid the biblical and theological groundwork that undergirds a vision for the virtual body of Christ, it is time to turn now to additional illustrations of how digital tools are already being used to enhance the power of the virtual body to better minister to those who need it most.

Since I have been awakened to the healing power of the virtual body of Christ, I have paid close attention to how people interact in the online social networks I am a part of. I am connected via online networks with many people who are part of the same community of faith as I am, and I am often struck by how much more I know about those same people's joys and sorrows from my virtual connections with them than I know about most fellow church members to whom I am not connected to online. Now this could be because I have not taken enough advantage of face-to-face opportunities at church to go deep into the lives of fellow members, but as author of *The Social Media Gospel* Meredith Gould proposes, it is important to acknowledge that getting to know fellow members at church takes time. When encouraging her readers to think about how online connections can enhance church-based relationships, Gould asks,

> How many times did you exchange a sign of peace with [others in church] before chatting with them after worship? How many conversations did it take before you exchanged personal contact information? How long did it take for you to then use that information to reach out? How long before anyone used it to invite you to participate in anything? If your experience has been anything like mine, it took a while to shift from exchanging pleasantries in the narthex to considering other congregants as friends.[5]

Once again, participating in the same virtual networks as others from my own church gives me a broader and deeper sense of the texture of these friends' daily lives. It keeps me much more plugged in to a friend's young son's daily radiation treatments for brain cancer and to the healing journey of another friend who was hospitalized recently but not on the congregational prayer list. That more and more sharing of life's joys and sorrows happens virtually means more and more opportunities for support, both in the virtual and in the material realm.

Like many churches of the twenty-first century, the church I attend is well aware that people are not as connected as they could be to one another. In part to address that issue, our church began training a few dozen of us in a practice of "courageous conversations," a practice of intentional one-on-one conversations where we dare to go deep and talk about what matters in our lives. Nearly everyone who participated in these conversations testified to being transformed by the time spent with other members they did not know well, invoking words like *sacred* and *holy* to describe the conversations. During our first summer of one-on-ones, those of us who were trained participated in over two hundred intentional conversations. Many of those sacred connections now continue in virtual spaces in addition to in-person connections at church and beyond. The virtual and material interactions mutually reinforce one another, strengthening the connections within the body of Christ. While digital critics in the Christian arena lament that church members allow Facebook rather than liturgy to establish the rituals that mark our lives,[6] my hope is that scholars and church leaders alike will come to understand social networks as more continuous than discontinuous with our material lives. Rather than persistent laments about the digital revolution, why not ask how churches might better utilize virtual spaces to enhance our ability to be the hands and feet of Christ in the world?

Increasing numbers of church communities have embraced the recognition that ours is a postwebsite world and are creatively and intentionally utilizing virtual connections to better be the body of Christ. One faith community that has tapped the potential for virtual connectivity in ways that have transformed their community is Granger Community Church in Indiana, a congregation that has been using an online tool called "The Table" since 2011. This customized social platform allows churches to create a number of interactive sites, from an online membership directory to interactive prayer walls where parishioners post joys and concerns. Enabling the church members to communicate more fully in virtual ways has been transforming this particular incarnation of the body of Christ in not-so-subtle ways. They no longer rely on outdated directories to put faces to names; instead, church members use a closed social network similar to Facebook as their directory, and names and faces are added as soon as they commit to being a part of the community. In addition, members utilize this social network in a number of important ways: the site has a "Serve App" where parishioners can post what they need (a ride to an appointment or a request for raking the lawn) as well as services they are willing to offer for free and even items they are giving away. Perhaps most importantly, there is a prayer wall where those who want to share joys and sorrows can do so.

One unexpected development from the Granger congregation's interaction via the Table has been that those who are dealing with a variety of serious issues are finding solace and support in making connections with those who share similar challenges. Once again, online social networks are places where weak ties are becoming strong ties. Granger Church Pastor Rob Wegner reports that through their prayer wall, a number of couples struggling with infertility issues have found one another and begun a support group. Connections that began virtually are now being strengthened by face-to-face interactions, and these relationships have been deeply comforting to those who share a struggle to have children.[7] This illustration of connections being forged among members of this particular church community highlights ways in which virtual connections within a congregation can lead to a decentering in how the ministry in and of the church is being carried out. With its own closed network for virtual communication, Granger Community Church has created the possibility of members connecting with one another without necessarily being dependent upon a pastor, staff member, or volunteer creating structured opportunities to do so.[8] Similar to what I have seen in my own experience with online networks, the virtual body of Christ is at work allowing the suffering of the members of the body to become more visible and providing support and comfort that may not have come (or come as easily or quickly) if left to in-person connections within the church community.

While social networks designed specifically for churches offer a number of powerful opportunities to be the body of Christ to one another, many churches and church leaders utilize existing social media sites for ministry. Drescher relates the story of how Kirk Smith, bishop of the Episcopal Diocese of Arizona, took to Facebook to share photos, videos, and notes about an immersion trip taken in 2010 by over two dozen bishops of the Episcopal Church to the borderlands between Arizona and Mexico. This trip followed on the heels of the state of Arizona passing a controversial law requiring law enforcement to question people about their immigration status if they believe there is reason to do so. The goal of the bishops' trip was to meet with migrants and borderland congregations to learn more about the challenges they face and also to demonstrate to migrants and the churches at the border that the wider church is committed to becoming more attentive to their suffering. Drescher also notes that the bishop's use of social media while on the border "offer[ed] a spiritual and ethical engagement that [brought] together digital and multiple face-to-face communities that would not otherwise cross paths."[9] Bishop Smith's physical presence among migrant communities was a tangible witness to those who fled their homes and made the often-harrowing trip across the border. One minister of a border community told him, "We're all like ghosts out here in the desert, floating around invisibly. . . . But when people come to see us here, they see not just ghosts, but . . .[l]iving beings. People on the same earth with them."[10] The bishops' visit helped communicate that those on the border are part of the church catholic and that the wider body of Christ not only hears their cries but is present with them—physically and virtually—amid their suffering.

In her analysis of the bishop's Facebook postings about the experience on the border, Drescher proposes that Bishop Smith's digital witness might even be read as a ceding of "institutional space to those on the further margins of [the church]."[11] In other words, the use of social media to witness to suffering on the border presents a decentered model of ministry where the words and images of those living on the border occupy a position of authority. Granted, the bishop is the one framing the stories, and Drescher realizes that critics might view these postings as a kind of click activism where followers of the bishop on social media feel like they are supporting migrant workers because they "liked" a picture or a post. In response to such critiques, Drescher suggests, I think rightly, that the fact that Smith is writing to an established community—the Episcopal Church he serves—is vital to seeing his witness as effective. "It allows that his digital presence moves beyond the mere witness of activism to an act of witness that genuinely strengthens the Church as a community of justice and hope."[12] To move from engaging on social media about the lives of those at the border to material support or even policy change at the state or national level is most certainly a challenge, but the digital engagement of these issues for the Episcopal Church in Arizona brings a new level of awareness, attention, and potentially action to often-invisible members of the body of Christ.

Limitations of and Challenges with the Virtual Body of Christ

Even with a both/and approach to the use of digital technology to augment face-to-face interactions of the body of Christ, there will still be times when virtual interactions with those who are suffering either will be inferior to face-to-face encounters or simply will not be possible. The university where I teach is still grieving the loss of a beloved Old Testament scholar and teacher who was forced into retirement by Alzheimer's disease. A couple short years after retirement, this award-winning former professor moved into a memory care facility. It was sad, cruel even, for one who loved words more than just about anything else in life, that words simply went away. For the first several months in the memory care facility, this friend and colleague would call me on his cell phone, and those conversations helped us maintain contact in between in-person visits. But as the disease progressed, he had less and less to do with digital devices. Family, friends, and colleagues had to visit him in person to communicate with him, and even then, communication was often strained. While it is the case that increasing numbers of people who are ill are receiving life-giving support through virtual forms of communication during the awful times, visits with my friend confronted me with the limits of virtual support for those who struggle with cognitive issues.

Even though Alzheimer's cut off most possibilities of virtual communication with our friend, it was nevertheless the case that a community of family, friends, colleagues, and former students formed a virtual network via e-mail, offering updates after each visit with him, sharing stories of what he enjoyed—whether it was reading from the Psalms, Annie Dillard, or Wendell Berry, or looking at scrapbooks of family pictures—and encouraging one another to keep visiting. It was another glimpse of how virtual connections can augment our in-person connections with one another to better support those in need of care.

The story of our struggle to support a dear friend with Alzheimer's raises the uncomfortable issue of how responses from individuals and communities can vary based on a number of factors, one of which is the social acceptability of the illness. In the movie version of Lisa Genova's novel *Still Alice*, a story about a Harvard professor turned Alzheimer's patient, Alice is exasperated with having to negotiate this loss of words and memory in a world that often does not understand her disease. "I just wish I had cancer instead!" she wails. As someone who lives with cancer, Alice's wish was initially jarring to hear. Clearly none of us wants to have cancer or any other serious illness. And as I have discussed in previous chapters, negotiating the world of the well when one is not well presents a host of difficult challenges, regardless of the diagnosis. Furthermore, both studies about and personal experiences of those who live with cancer suggest that gaps of understanding and degrees of acceptability still exist amid cancer diagnoses.[13] Yet Alice's cry suggests some diseases carry stigma that can make it harder for those who are ill to communicate what it is like to live with a particular disease as well as those who want to be supportive of those who are ill to provide comfort and support.

This point about the challenges of communicating about illnesses that often are accompanied by stigma was again brought home to me recently when I attended a forum at our church about mental illness. The presenter from the National Alliance on Mental Illness (NAMI) addressed the issue of stigma that is still often attached to mental illness in ways that differ from physical illnesses. "Have you ever seen a CaringBridge site for someone struggling with mental illness?" she asked. This was another statement that was challenging to hear as someone who has benefitted from so much support via this online network. The fact that I have not seen a CaringBridge site for someone with mental illness also reveals an important truth about how our society supports (or struggles to support) those who live with such illnesses. Womanist theologian Monica Coleman writes about the stigma associated with mental illness and the isolation it can induce. Coleman suggests that stigma pushes people who live with mental illness "into a silence that quickly becomes shame. When few people are talking about what they live with, it's easy to think you're alone."[14] In response to this isolation, Coleman, herself a pastor, proposes that communities like the church can be vital spaces of support for those living with mental illness. "The irony is that community is the best antidote for isolation; acceptance is the best cure for silence and shame; fellowship is the best remedy for grief."[15] But of course, support from other people can be excruciatingly difficult to seek out, as Coleman, who lives with mental illness, knows firsthand. As church communities become more responsive to the needs of those with mental illness, it will be important for these communities to work with those who live with such illnesses to figure out whether and how virtual connections can enhance what it means to be the body of Christ in ways that are supportive.

Other persons who often have limited use of digital technology are those who are blind or visually impaired. While assistive technology exists that reads screen content out loud or magnifies the content on screens for users to better access materials digitally,[16] it is nevertheless the case that not all persons who are blind or visually impaired have access to such technology. Assistive technology is often expensive, and it continues to change rapidly, making it more challenging for those who need assistance to navigate such sight-dependent technologies.[17] The digitalization of everything from toasters to coffee makers to electric blankets, where reading screen displays is necessary to operate the product, means that those who are visually impaired face new obstacles to functioning independently in our digital age. Once again, church communities need to be cognizant of how their use of digital tools affects members of the community whose disabilities make it more difficult to interact with some forms of digital technology.

Yet another limitation for virtual connection and support that must be addressed is limited access to online networks due to socioeconomic factors. As discussed in the second chapter, for all the ways cyberspaces have the potential to reach further and more equitably than ever before, those with scarce resources likely will not experience the embrace from the virtual body of Christ due to lack of their own virtual presence and connection to online networks. Meanwhile, those without strong virtual connections still get sick. The National Cancer Institute reports that those living in poverty are diagnosed with more advanced cancer and have lower rates of survival than those living in more affluent communities.[18] In a recent study on those living in poverty in urban areas who also live with advanced cancer, oncology nurses report not just on frequent lack of supportive family structures but also on the prevalence of other traumas (violence against themselves or close family members, wartime military service, etc.) that compound the trauma of dealing with their life-threatening illness. The nurses insist that "understanding the everyday lives of patients is necessary to develop realistic and practical self-care plans and to identify needed community resources."[19] Being the hands and feet of Christ calls on Christians to attend to the shouts of the Bartimaeuses of our time; but even more, we are called to be attentive to those whose trauma is so great that their calls are not heard. In her powerful essay on race and medicine in the African American community, womanist ethicist Emilie Townes argues for the centrality of lament as a practice of and for communities struggling with access to adequate health care and other resources necessary for health. Issues of illness affect us all, Townes points out, which is why she believes "that *communal* lament can best help us get at the complexities of these issues."[20] Religious communities that lift their collective voices in lament over lack of resources and limited access to medical care will not just increase attention toward these issues and the people they affect but will also help those who live in such conditions voice their own hardships and clear some space for hope. Collective lament helps facilitate visions of collective hope in the vision of health and wholeness of the gospel message. Townes insists that this hope "will order and shape our lives in ways that are not always predictable, not always safe, and rarely conventional."[21] The virtual body of Christ must also be a space where such communal laments are raised and attention is directed to those whose virtual presence is harder to detect due to difficulty communicating, stigma, or lack of access to virtual networks.

In addition to the above-mentioned limitations of virtual connectivity to enhance support for those who suffer, it is vital that church communities are also clear-eyed about some of the challenges raised by virtual communication. As many church communities are already well aware, one important issue involves respecting the privacy of those who are going through tough times. In 1996, the

Health Insurance Portability and Accountability Act (HIPAA) became a federal law. This law was designed to protect the privacy of individuals' health-related information. Even though churches are not "health plans" or "health-care providers" and are not "covered entities" according to the rule, the passage of this act has nevertheless prompted further thinking among and within church communities about how a person's health-related information is communicated in public ways.[22] Churches have become more aware of privacy issues and often take concrete steps (such as making sure approval is secured from a particular individual before putting any names on prayer lists) to respect the privacy of members.

No doubt, some of the concern by church leaders about utilizing online social networks as vehicles for support of those who suffer has to do with the incredibly public nature of social media as well as the demonstrated ease of sharing another person's information, possibly without their consent. An update posted by an individual on Facebook about a health-related issue can quickly be shared far beyond the individual's own network, and this can lead to challenges about consent of having such information shared. Utilizing a closed online social network like the Table or a closed Facebook group for a church community can help mitigate that concern. At the same time, all of us who participate in online social networks know that the often-inattentive ways in which people engage with social media increases the risk that people could cut and paste an update even in a closed network and share it without permission. In addition, the ubiquitous practice of commenting on posts may heighten the risk that members within the closed network may make a poorly worded or insensitive comment on a post by someone who is sharing difficult health news while in a particularly vulnerable state, therefore easily wounding them by displays of insensitivity.

On the other hand, social media sites also can be places where some people overshare, providing updates multiple times a day or posting rants about a particular issue about which they are passionate, leading to frustration and the possible tuning out of other participants within the social network. Churches hosting closed social media sites would do well to offer etiquette guidelines for using such sites as well as to have staff members who oversee the sites and who will remind participants of the guidelines of how to utilize such sites. Several great resources exist, such as Meredith Gould's *The Social Media Gospel: Sharing the Good News in New Ways*, that offer strategies on how to frame churches' use of online social media tools for ministry.

What I am suggesting is that churches can play potentially critical roles in educating people on how to utilize online social media resources to better care for one another and to help people become more proficient in avoiding some of the pitfalls often encountered in online social networks. In addition, I encourage pastors, parish nurses, and other church staff or volunteers who work with those who are hospitalized, ill, or others who experience a life-altering event where support is needed to include options for communication about health issues with family, friends, and the church community in their pastoral or congregational care conversations. When people experience a sudden, serious diagnosis or life-altering accident, one of the many issues that they will face is whether and how they will share their news with others in their lives. There are many options, ranging from keeping the news extremely private to sharing it widely via social media, and I think many people would benefit from talking through these options with a pastor or parish nurse. More support for us while we're suffering is possible when news is shared widely with tools like CaringBridge or Facebook or e-mail, but liabilities also exist with each option. I have written elsewhere about potential advantages and disadvantages of using a site like CaringBridge.[23] My knowledge of how these various options for sharing health news work has come through the trial and error of living with a serious illness and trying out various ways of communicating how I am doing with those who care about me. Pastoral care that includes conversations and even shares resources about pros and cons of different approaches could be very valuable for those who find that their lives are being undone. Again, it is another way in which the church can be the body of Christ for the weakest among us.

Expanding the Boundaries of the Virtual Body of Christ

While Christians have long imagined the body of Christ in universal terms, that universality has still had a sense of "boundedness." The body of Christ is a community of persons who confess belief in the triune God and become members of the body through the sacrament of baptism. To be part of the body of Christ, then, is to be bound in particular ways to the beliefs and practices of the Christian community, the church. At the same time, the emphasis on the catholicity of the church gestures to an openness, a sense of not being confined to descriptions of the church that focus narrowly on its boundaries. As theologian Daniel Migliore points out, "The church does not 'have' the living Christ at its disposal or 'possess' the Spirit as something under its control. Rather, the church is called to participate in the mission of Christ and the Spirit."[24] The "true" church, according to Migliore, is not only where the gospel is preached and sacraments are administered, but it is also where the hungry are fed, the sick are comforted, and the imprisoned are visited (Matt 25:31). In other words, the mission of Christ and the Spirit is in ministering to the weakest among us, and following that command consistently takes the church beyond comfortable boundaries and into spaces beyond.

As I have relayed through the pages of this book, I have experienced what it is like to be among "the weakest" members of the body. I have been the recipient of so many gifts of comfort, support, love, and care from a communion of saints much more vast than I could have ever imagined prior to getting sick. And that communion of saints includes many members of the church universal, but there are also saints in that communion from outside Christianity, whether they be Hindu, Buddhist, Jewish, Native American, or of no faith at all. My social networks reflect a growing reality for twenty-first-century persons: that our networks are more diverse than they used to be. And with the expansion of our social networks to cyberspaces, the potential for networks with diverse religious beliefs continues to increase. The expanding virtual network that has supported me and my family over the past seven years includes persons from multiple religious traditions, and many of those who are outside the boundaries of the body of Christ have offered life-giving support and care to us as well. How, then, does that reality shape this vision of the virtual body of Christ that I am proposing? How far does the bounded openness of the church catholic extend?

In responding to these questions, I want to avoid what comparative theologian John Thatamanil says is bearing false witness against our neighbor when we Christians attempt to include persons who are not Christian into our already-determined Christian frameworks (like the body of Christ).[25] When my friend who is Hindu visits his temple and offers prayers on my behalf, or when my friend who is Native American invites me into her office to perform a sage smudging for me, or when a friend who is Buddhist dedicates his meditation session to my well being, I want to affirm that these are gifts of prayer and healing that come to me as gifts from traditions of which I am not a part. And even though I cannot claim an insider's understanding of any of these religious practices, I am deeply grateful for these spiritual gifts of support and energy and healing. Because of those gifts, these friends are part of a communion of saints who have borne witness to my suffering and cared for the weakest in their midst. As I said in my conversion story at the beginning of the book, I see these friends, all of whom are outside the body of Christ, working in tandem with that body to care for those who need it.

When it comes to my agnostic Jewish friend who entered Christian places of worship throughout Israel and got down on her knees and prayed to Jesus, however, the story takes a different turn. While this friend also prayed regularly for me at her synagogue, her literal adoption of a prayer stance of a religious other, not to mention directing her prayers to one her tradition does not regard as divine, requires a somewhat different response to whether or not my friend who is Jewish was, during these moments of prayer, part of the body of Christ. If participation in the body of Christ requires ascent to belief in the trinitarian God and the seal of the cross of Christ in baptism, then clearly my friend is outside the bounds of that vision of the body of Christ. If, however, a vision of bounded *openness* of the body of Christ includes space for those religious others who voluntarily enter that space and participate in particular bounded practices and thereby embody the command to specially attend to the weakest among us, it seems possible for me to claim her, however briefly, as part of an expanded version of the body of Christ.

As I have searched various theological lexicons for language to capture this gift of healing prayer performed on my behalf by my dear colleague, I have not yet located terminology up to the task of describing my friend. The terms "multiple religious belonging" or "religious hybridity" are becoming more common as scholars address the reality of persons who practice more than one religious tradition simultaneously. But neither term seems an appropriate fit for my friend. She has no interest in any regular Christian practice; in fact, Christian places of worship are often difficult places for her to be. Her act is more an act of religious boundary crossing for the sake of the neighbor in need. It is a selfless, cruciform act for the sake of a friend.

My testimony to the supportive, healing power of the virtual body of Christ ends here, with this story of a friend who willingly stepped inside the boundaries of the body of Christ in order to pray for healing for me. As I testify in the story of my conversion to the power of the virtual body of Christ, I am quite confident that this boundary-crossing act by my Jewish friend would not have happened without the virtual network that was created in response to my diagnosis of stage IV cancer. The opportunities my friend and I have had to communicate virtually after my diagnosis led to deeper expressions of vulnerability and conversations about prayer and faith and hope than any face-to-face conversation between us ever had. And as Christians continue to explore how the body of Christ is present virtually, we will need to continue to develop a wider lexicon of terms to talk about participation in the body of Christ as its boundaries continue to stretch and expand in new directions.

Ours is a world being remade by digital technology and virtual interactions. This new world brings with it liabilities and losses. At the same time, new ways of being connected to one another are emerging, and with them, new possibilities for supporting one another during the worst times of our lives. Before my cancer diagnosis, I never would have believed such a claim. But I am here to testify to the power of virtual support, not just for the present but for the past and the future as well. It is important for Christians to recognize that the body of Christ has always been a virtual body and that, in this digital age, incarnational living must be understood as incorporating virtual as well as face-to-face interactions. In this new world, the church is poised to play a countercultural role in helping all of us who are constantly tempted to distraction by our digital devices to learn to develop patterns of paying close attention to the distractions that matter most, especially as they involve our neighbors who are hurting. Through the church's embrace of the emerging benefits of digital connectivity, Christian communities can continue to live into the call to be the body of Christ with and for one another and the world with our deepest attention reserved for those who need it most. Thanks be to God for this new tool of ministry.

SMS

Discussion Questions

Introduction

1. Before being diagnosed with advanced-stage cancer, Thompson considered herself a digital skeptic, someone who sees more problems than possibilities with digital technology. How would you describe your view of the technology increasingly present in our lives?

2. What is it, exactly, that causes Thompson's conversion to a different relationship to technology? Have you witnessed what she calls "the virtual body of Christ" in your life or the lives of others you know?

3. Thompson proposes that connections forged with help from digital technology can lead us to rethink the boundaries of the body of Christ, as her example of her colleague who prayed for her in Israel suggests. How do you see technology changing the ways we think about the church?

Chapter 1

1. According to Thompson, human history is also a history of technological innovation that has brought revolutionary changes to how human beings live. Weighing in on current debates about whether we are primarily shaped by or shapers of technology, Thompson sides with those who view technology as a tool that can be used by humans for good or for ill. Which side of the debate makes more sense to you and why?

2. Thompson believes that online social networks are not necessarily less real or less important than social networks that depend upon face-to-face interactions. Why does she believe this? Are you with her? Why or why not?

3. Just as technology continues to change rapidly, so does the language we use to talk about technology. Are we having experiences via digital technology in cyberspace? In the virtual world? Do we live our lives primarily in augmented reality? What language makes the most sense to you to capture what's going on with the current digital revolution?

Chapter 2

1. Thompson suggests that the Apostle Paul utilizes the common ancient metaphor of the body to envision what it means to be church, but he does so in uncommon ways. How does his use of this image for the church indicate how the church operates in a distinct way from how society tends to operate?

2. While Christians understand Paul as pastor and leader of several first-century congregations, Thompson wants us to consider the fact that he was present "virtually," primarily through his letters, and that such virtual communication had very real consequences for how communities embodied church. How does this way of seeing Paul's relationship with those early church communities affect your view of what it means to be church?

3. Thompson also proposes that thinking about the church as "the virtual body of Christ" relates to claims from the time of Paul onward that there is not just the local church but also the church universal (referred to in the creeds as the "catholic church"). How do you think about the universality of the church? Are there ways to hold on to this idea while simultaneously embracing the incredible diversity of global Christianity?

4. Thompson draws on sociological research to highlight the importance of weak as well as strong ties in our social networks, whether they are online or in-person. What are some examples of weak ties playing a significant role in your own life? Do you believe that both weak and strong ties can be cultivated and/or maintained with the help of online social networks? Why or why not?

Chapter 3

1. What do you think are some of the most important aspects of the claim that Christianity is an incarnational religion? Why do some Christian thinkers worry that digital technology is leading us toward *dis*incarnated living? How valid are these concerns in your mind?

2. Why does Thompson believe it is so important to see the "virtual" and "real" worlds as more continuous than discontinuous? How does she draw on her own experiences of being really sick to support the view that virtual communication can facilitate being the hands and feet of Christ to those who live with serious illness? Does she persuade you on the incarnational potential for virtual support? Why or why not?

3. Is the formation of "an incarnational theology for a digital age" a worthwhile project? If so, what other features might you add to Thompson's list of four attributes of such a theology?

Chapter 4

1. To what extent do you agree with Thompson's claim that "attentiveness is under threat" in our current age? How much are our digital devices to blame for that inattentiveness? How do you personally attempt to deal with the constant temptation to be distracted by digital devices?

2. Thompson suggests that in the story of Jesus's healing of Bartimaeus in Mark 10, we have a model for sustained attention and its healing effects. What sticks with you most from this story? How does the story encourage you to think about being attentive in our current context to those who are hurting?

3. Thompson proposes that a key function of Christian worship is to cultivate attentiveness toward God and one another, with special attention toward those who are hurting. Where have you seen the church do this well? When has the church fallen short of cultivating such attentiveness? How might the church better utilize—and shape how its members utilize—technology to attend to the deep hurts that exist within—and beyond—the local and universal church?

Chapter 5

1. If "ours is a postwebsite world," how might the church go beyond digital strategies to facilitate connections within and beyond the church community?

2. Thompson acknowledges several important limitations when it comes to utilizing technology as a tool to support those who need it. Are there other limitations you would add?

3. What is the most important takeaway for you from this book? Thompson concludes this chapter with a prayer of thanksgiving for digital connectivity. Has this book encouraged you to reconsider the potential of technology to help the church better be the body of Christ? Why or why not?

Notes

Introduction

1. Cathy Caruth, "Preface," in *Trauma: Explorations in Memory* (Baltimore: Johns Hopkins University Press, 1995).

2. Annette Baier, "Trust and Antitrust," *Ethics* 96, no. 2 (Jan., 1986): 235.

3. John Thatamanil, *The Immanent Divine: God, Creation, and the Human Predicament* (Minneapolis: Fortress Press, 2006), xi–xii.

4. Margaret Wertheim, *The Pearly Gates of Cyberspace: A History of Space from Dante to the Internet* (New York: W. W. Norton & Co., 2000), 285.

5. Rev. Matthew Senf, e-mail correspondence, November 10, 2014.

6. Jason Byassee, "Digital Church Conference Presentation," New Media Project, last modified February 2013, accessed July 28, 2015, http://www.cpx .cts.edu/newmedia/resources/digital-church-conference-video.

1. Imagine That

1. Steven Harnad, "Post-Gutenberg Galaxy: The Fourth Revolution in the Means of Production in Knowledge," *Public-Access Computer Systems Review* 2, no. 1 (1991): 39–53, http://users.ecs.soton.ac.uk/harnad/Papers/Harnad/harnad 91.postgutenberg.html.

2. Elizabeth Palermo, "Who Invented the Printing Press?" February 25, 2014, LiveScience, accessed February 27 2016, http://www.livescience.com/43639 -who-invented-the-printing-press.html.

3. Nicholas G. Carr, *The Shallows: What the Internet Is Doing to Our Brains* (New York: W.W. Norton and Co., 2011), 55.

4. Neil Postman, *Amusing Ourselves to Death: Public Discourse in the Age of Show Business* (New York: Penguin, 2005), 8.

5. Mike Ives, "Boom in Mining Rare Earths Poses Mounting Toxic Risks," Yale Environment 360, online publication of the Yale School of Forestry, accessed August 5, 2015, http://e360.yale.edu/feature/boom_in_mining_rare _earths_poses_mounting_toxic_risks/2614/. See also organizations like Enough: the Project to End Genocide and Crimes against Humanity and their advocacy for US government policies that will support certification for conflict-free electronics. Currently communities in the Democratic Republic of Congo experience rape and murder within their communities in order for government and militia forces to profit from the mining of conflict minerals. See http://www .enoughproject.org/conflict-minerals for more information on how to support conflict free electronics.

6. "Unsafe Driving in the Cell Phone Era," Cellphone Safety, accessed August 5, 2015, http://www.cellphonesafety.org/vehicular/era.htm.

7. Janet Raloff, "Cell Phones: Feds Probing Impact," *Science News*, September 14, 2009, accessed August 5, 2015, https://www.sciencenews.org/blog /science-public/cell-phones-feds-probing-health-impacts.

8. See Robert Putnam, *Bowling Alone: The Collapse and Revival of American Community* (New York: Simon and Schuster, 2000); see also Keith Hampton et al., "Social Isolation and New Technology," the 2009 Pew Research Study on "Social Isolation and New Technology," *Pew Research Center*, last modified November 4, 2009, http://www.pewinternet.org/2009/11/04/social-isolation-and -new-technology/.

9. Carr, *The Shallows*; see particularly chapter 7, "The Juggler's Brain," 115–43.

10. James Davison Hunter, *To Change the World: The Irony, Tragedy, and Possibility of Christianity in the Late Modern World* (Oxford, UK: Oxford University Press, 2010), 222.

11. Carr, *The Shallows*, 46.

12. Ibid., 224.

13. Gerard Goggin and Christopher Newell, *Digital Disability: The Social Construction of Disability in New Media* (Lanham, MD: Rowman and Littlefield Publishers, Inc., 2003), 8.

14. Ibid., 11.

15. Carr, *The Shallows*, 47.

16. Steven Gray, "What Obama's Election Really Means to Black America," *Time Magazine Online*, November 6, 2008, accessed August 4, 2015, http://content.time.com/time/nation/article/0,8599,1857222,00.html.

17. Zachary Davies Boren, "There are Officially More Mobile Devices in the World Than People," *The Independent*, October 7, 2014, http://www.independent.co.uk/life-style/gadgets-and-tech/news/there-are-officially-more-mobile-devices-than-people-in-the-world-9780518.html.

18. Roberto A. Ferdman, "4.4 Billion People around the World Still Don't Have Internet. Here's Where They Live," *The Washington Post*, October 2, 2014, http://www.washingtonpost.com/blogs/wonkblog/wp/2014/10/02/4-4-billion-people-around-the-world-still-dont-have-internet-heres-where-they-live/.

19. Doug Gross, "Google Boss: Entire World Will Be Online by 2020," *CNN*, April 15, 2013, http://www.cnn.com/2013/04/15/tech/web/eric-schmidt-internet/.

20. David Krackhardt, "The Strength of Strong Ties: The Importance of Philos in Organizations" in *Networks and Organizations: Structure, Form, and Action*, ed. N. Nohria, et al. (Boston, MA: Harvard Business School Press, 1992), 216–39.

21. See Parker J. Palmer, *Healing the Heart of Democracy: The Courage to Create a Politics Worthy of the Human Spirit* (San Francisco: Jossey-Bass, 2010), 171.

22. Malcolm Gladwell, "Small Change: Why the Revolution Will Not Be Tweeted," *New Yorker*, Oct. 4, 2010, accessed July 10, 2015, http://www.newyorker.com/magazine/2010/10/04/small-change-3.

23. Ibid.

24. See Mark Granovetter, "The Strength of Weak Ties," *American Journal of Sociology* 78, no. 6 (1973): 1360–80.

25. Michael Frost, *Incarnate: The Body of Christ in an Age of Disengagement* (Downers Grove, IL: InterVarsity Press, 2014), 120, 122.

26. Stanley Hauerwas, "Salvation and Health: Why Medicine Needs the Church," *On Moral Medicine: Theological Perspectives in Medical Ethics*, ed. Stephen Lammers, et al., 2nd ed. (Grand Rapids, MI: William B. Eerdmans, 1998), 81.

27. Herbert Ruffin, "Black Lives Matter: The Growth of a New Social Justice Movement," BlackPast.org: An Online Reference Guide to African American History, accessed January 8, 2016, http://www.blackpast.org/perspectives/black-lives-matter-growth-new-social-justice-movement.

28. See Lilly Worknah, "11 Big Accomplishments Black Activists Achieved in 2015," *Huffington Post*, December 22, 2015, http://www.huffingtonpost.com/entry/11-big-accomplishments-black-activists-achieved-in-2015_567996bae4b0b958f6583320.

29. Granovetter, "The Strength of Weak Ties," 1360–80.

30. Zeynep Tufekci, "What Gladwell Gets Wrong: The Real Problem Is Scale Mismatch (Plus, Weak and Strong Ties Are Complementary and Supportive)," Technosociology: Our Tools, Ourselves, last modified September 27, 2010, accessed July 24, 2015, http://technosociology.org/?p=178.

31. Mary Evelyn, "That Time the Internet Saved My Son's Life," *What Do You Do, Dear?*, last revised October 15, 2014, http://www.whatdoyoudodear.com/time-internet-saved-sons-life/.

32. Ibid.

33. Howard Rheingold, *The Virtual Community: Homesteading on the Electronic Frontier*, rev. ed. (Boston: MIT Press, 2000), 4–5.

34. "Part III: Social Networking Site Users Have More Friends and More Close Friends," Pew Research Center, "Social Networking Sites and Our Lives," June 2011, accessed August 11, 2015, http://www.pewinternet.org/2011/06/16/part-3-social-networking-site-users-have-more-friends-and-more-close-friends.

35. Reed, *Digitized Lives*, 20.

36. William Gibson, *Neuromancer* (New York: Ace Books, 1984), 51.

37. Reed, *Digitized Lives*, 17–18.

38. Reed, *Digitized Lives*, 21.

39. Tom Boellstorff, *Coming of Age in Second Life: An Anthropologist Explores the Virtually Human* (Princeton, NJ: Princeton University Press, 2008), 5.

40. Heather A. Horst and Daniel Miller, ed., *Digital Anthropology* (London: Bloomsbury Academic, 2013), 4.

41. Boellstorff, *Coming of Age in Second Life*, 21.

42. Ibid., 5.

43. www.augmentedreality.org, accessed May 14, 2016.

44. "The End of See One, Do One, Teach One," *OHSU Bridges Magazine*, August 2009, 8–10, http://www.ohsu.edu/xd/education/schools/school-of-med icine/loader.cfm?csModule=security/getfile&pageid=757372.

45. Ibid.

46. Hazel Davis, "Enhancing the Human Race: Augmented Reality," *The Telegraph*, December 20, 2013, http://www.telegraph.co.uk/sponsored/health /scientific-breakthroughs/10523379/augmented-reality-medicine.html.

2. The Body of Christ Has Always Been and Will Always Be a Virtual Body

1. For an accessible presentation of "new perspectives on Paul," see John Gager, *Reinventing Paul* (Oxford: Oxford University Press, 2002).

2. Ignatius, "Letter to the Ephesians," chap. 12, accessed May 14, 2016, http://www.earlychristianwritings.com/text/ignatius-ephesians-lightfoot.html; Dionysius of Corinth, "Letter to the Romans," chap. 3, accessed May 14, 2016, http://www.earlychristianwritings.com/text/dionysius.html.

3. James W. Thompson, *The Church according to Paul: Rediscovering the Community Conformed to Christ* (Grand Rapids, MI: Baker Academic, 2014), 16.

4. Ibid., 27.

5. Elizabeth Drescher, *Tweet If You Heart Jesus: Practicing Church in the Digital Reformation* (Harrisburg, PA: Morehouse Publishing, 2011), 85.

6. Dennis Duling, "Paul's Aegean Network: The Strength of Strong Ties," *Biblical Theology Bulletin* 43 (2013): 142.

7. Drescher, *Tweet If You Heart Jesus*, 79.

8. Ibid.

9. Michelle V. Lee, *Paul, the Stoics, and the Body of Christ*, Society for New Testament Studies Series (Cambridge: Cambridge University Press, 2006), 9.

10. Margeret Mitchell, *Paul and the Rhetoric of Reconciliation* (Louisville, KY: Westminster John Knox Press, 1993), 147.

11. Lee, *Paul, the Stoics, and the Body of Christ*, 87–88.

12. Thompson, *The Church according to Paul*, 70.

13. Lee, *Paul, the Stoics, and the Body of Christ*, 120.

14. Ibid., 142.

15. See Sarah Ruden's *Paul among the People: The Apostle Reinterpreted and Reimagined in His Own Time* (New York: Pantheon Books, 2010), 85, for the point about head coverings for virtuous women, and *The Lutheran Study Bible* (Minneapolis: Augsburg Fortress, 2009), 1887, for the point about women's hairstyles.

16. Commentary on 1 Corinthians 14 in the *Lutheran Study Bible*, 1891.

17. Jouette M. Bassler, "1 Corinthians," *Women's Bible Commentary, Twentieth Anniversary Edition*, ed. Carol A. Newsom, et al. (Louisville, KY: Westminster John Knox Press, 2012), 563.

18. Guillermo Hansen, "The Networking of Differences That Makes a Difference: Theology and Unity of the Church," *Dialog: A Journal of Theology* 51, no. 1 (Spring 2012): 36.

19. Lee, *Paul, the Stoics, and the Body of Christ*, 144.

20. Richard A. Horseley, ed., *Paul and Politics* (Harrisburg, PA: Trinity, 2000), 92.

21. Hansen, "The Networking of Differences That Makes a Difference: Theology and Unity of the Church," 35.

22. Lee, *Paul, the Stoics, and the Body of Christ*, 148.

23. Michael J. Gorman, *Apostle of the Crucified Lord: A Theological Introduction to Paul's Letters* (Grand Rapids, MI: William B. Eerdmans Publishing Company, 2004), 272.

24. Lee, *Paul, the Stoics, and the Body of Christ*, 142.

25. Hansen, "The Networking of Differences That Makes a Difference," 36.

26. Thompson, *The Church according to Paul*, 197.

27. Gorman, *Apostle of the Crucified Lord*, 273.

28. Thompson, *The Church according to Paul*, 175.

29. Dennis C. Duling, "Paul's Aegean Network: The Strength of Strong Ties," *Biblical Theology Bulletin* 43, no. 3 (2013): 138.

30. Ibid., 142.

31. Ibid., 143.

32. Ibid., 146.

33. Jason Byassee, "For Virtual Theological Education," *Faith and Leadership*, last modified March 2, 2011, http://www.faithandleadership.com/blog/03-02-2011/jason-byassee-for-virtual-theological-education.

34. It is beyond the scope of this project to explore how Paul's encounter on the road to Damascus is interpreted. Paul's claims in 1 Corinthians 15:8 that the risen Christ "appeared" to him, and in Galatians 1:15-16 that God was pleased "to reveal his Son" to him, are interpreted by some to mean that Paul saw the (spiritual body of the) resurrected Christ, while others suggest that such appearances and revelations were primarily auditory or received internally. For a robust discussion of the options, see Gerald Collins, "The Appearances of the Risen Christ: A Lexical-Exegetical Examination of St. Paul and Other Witnesses," *Irish Theological Quarterly* 79, no. 2 (2014): 128–43.

35. Drescher, *Tweet If You Heart Jesus*, 80.

36. Byassee, "For Virtual Theological Education."

37. Horst and Miller, *Digital Anthropology*, 13.

38. Drescher, *Tweet If You Heart Jesus*, 80–2.

39. Gorman, *Apostle of the Crucified Lord*, 274.

40. Drescher, *Tweet If You Heart Jesus*, 84.

41. Thompson, *The Church according to Paul*, 176–82.

42. Ibid., 197.

43. Gorman, *Apostle of the Crucified Lord*, 474.

44. E. Elizabeth Johnson, "Ephesians," *Women's Bible Commentary*, 3rd ed. (Louisville, KY: Westminster John Knox Press, 2012), 578.

45. Commentary on Colossians 3:18–4:1, in the *Lutheran Study Bible*, 1940.

46. Gorman, *Apostle of the Crucified Lord*, 499.

47. Johnson, *Women's Bible Commentary*, 578.

48. Gorman, *Apostle of the Crucified Lord*, 518–19.

49. The initial Nicene Creed from 325 CE did not include any reference to the church. In 381, at the First Council of Constantinople, the creed was expanded to include reference to the catholic church; see Mark A. Noll, *Turning Points: Decisive Moments in the History of Christianity*, 2nd ed. (Grand Rapids, MI: Baker Academic, 2000), 57.

50. Noll, *Turning Points*, 43.

51. Wolfhart Pannenberg, "Foundation Documents of the Faith: The Place of Creeds in Christianity Today," *The Expository Times* 91, no. 11 (December 1979): 328–32.

52. Pannenberg, "Foundation Documents of the Faith," 330.

53. Pannenberg cites dialogue between Roman Catholic and Orthodox Churches in the late twentieth century, "Foundation Documents of the Faith," 331.

54. Jaroslav Pelikan, interview by Krista Tippet, "The Need for Creeds," October 22, 2009, transcript, https://www.onbeing.org/program/need-creeds /transcript/1291.

55. Hansen, "The Networking of Differences That Makes a Difference," 33.

56. Ibid., 40–41.

3. Incarnational Living in the Digital Age

1. Sallie McFague, *The Body of God: An Ecological Theology* (Minneapolis: Fortress Press, 1993), 14.

2. Ibid.

3. C. S. Lewis, *The Four Loves* (Boston: Mariner Books, 1971), 109.

4. See an expanded presentation of Luther's theology of the cross in my *Crossing the Divide: Luther, Feminism, and the Cross* (Minneapolis: Fortress Press, 2004), especially chapter 1.

5. See my discussion of feminist critiques of Luther's view of sin in chapter 4 of Ibid.

6. James Davison Hunter, *To Change the World: The Irony, Tragedy, and Possibility of Christianity in the Late Modern World* (Oxford, UK: Oxford University Press, 2010).

7. Ibid., 238.

8. Michael Frost, *Incarnate: The Body of Christ in an Age of Disengagement* (Downers Grove, IL: InterVarsity Press, 2014), 9.

9. Ibid.

10. Ibid., 24; statistics from "Social Media, Social Life: How Teens View Their Digital Lives," *Commonsense Media*, June 26, 2012, https://www.common sensemedia.org/research/social-media-social-life-how-teens-view-their-digital -lives.

11. Frost, *Incarnate*, 28.

12. Kathryn Reklis, "X-Reality and the Incarnation," New Media Project, May 10, 2012, http://www.cpx.cts.edu/newmedia/findings/essays/x-reality-and -the-incarnation.

13. For stories on people who died because their obsession with video games led them to neglect their bodily needs, see Gillian Mohney, "Video Game Leads to Life-Threatening Condition for Gamer," ABC News, December 12, 2013, http://abcnews.go.com/Health/video-game-leads-life-threatening-condition-gamer/story?id=21182106.

14. Reklis, "X-Reality and the Incarnation."

15. Ibid.

16. Hauerwas, "Salvation and Health," 387–88.

17. Ibid.

18. Arthur Frank, "The Body's Problem with Illness," *The Body Reader: Essential Social and Cultural Readings*, ed. Lisa Jean Moore and Mary Kosut (New York: New York University Press, 2010), 32.

19. Ibid., 38.

20. Anatole Broyard, *Intoxicated by My Illness: And Other Writings on Life and Death*, comp. and ed. Alexandra Broyard (New York: Clarkson N. Potter, 1992), 23, quoted in Frank, "The Body's Problem with Illness," 38.

21. Hauerwas, "Salvation and Health," 79.

22. Ibid., 82.

23. Ibid., 72.

24. Frost, *Incarnate*, 30.

25. Lilian Calles Barger, *Eve's Revenge: Women and a Spirituality of the Body* (Grand Rapids, MI: Brazos, 2003), 96.

26. David Benner, *Presence and Encounter: The Sacramental Possibilities of Everyday Life* (Grand Rapids, MI: Brazos Press, 2014), 78.

27. Theresa of Avila, *The Life of St. Theresa of Avila*, trans. David Lewis (New York: Cosmoclassics, 2006), 60.

28. Martin Luther King Jr., *The Autobiography of Martin Luther King, Jr.*, ed. Clayborne Carson (New York: IPM/Warner Books, 2001), chap. 8, https://swap.stanford.edu/20141218230026/http://mlk-kpp01.stanford.edu/kingweb/publications/autobiography/chp_8.htm.

29. "Bitch slapped by the Spirit" is her actual claim. See Nadia Bolz-Weber, *Pastrix: The Cranky, Beautiful Faith of a Sinner and Saint* (Nashville: Jericho Books, 2014), 104.

30. Meredith Gould, *The Social Media Gospel: Sharing the Good News in New Ways* (Collegeville, MN: Liturgical Press, 2013), 8. Used by permission.

31. Andrew Byers, *TheoMedia: The Media of God and the Digital Age* (Eugene, OR: Cascade Press, 2013), 180.

32. Lilian Calles Barger writes, "In cyberspace accountability is practically nonexistent. We can ask, 'Who is my neighbor?' and there is no answer. In cyberspace we can remain anonymous and disconnected while retaining the illusion that we 'know' one another." See Barger, *Eve's Revenge*, 97.

33. Howard Thurman, *Jesus and the Disinherited* (Boston: Beacon Press, 1976), 89.

4. Attending to the Weakest Members of the Body in the Digital Age

1. "Barney McCoy Publishes New Digital Distractions Survey," *University of Nebraska–Lincoln: College of Journalism and Mass Communicatoins,* accessed January 20, 2016, http://journalism.unl.edu/news/barney-mccoy-publishes -new-digital-distractions-study.

2. Kathryn Reklis, "X-Reality and the Incarnation," New Media Project, May 10, 2012, http://www.cpx.cts.edu/newmedia/findings/essays/x-reality-and -the-incarnation.

3. James Davison Hunter, *To Change the World: The Irony, Tragedy, and Possibility of Christianity in the Late Modern World* (Oxford, UK: Oxford University Press, 2010), 209.

4. J. Marshall Jenkins, *A Wakeful Faith: Spiritual Practice in the Real World* (Nashville: Upper Room Publications, 2000), 1.

5. Leighton Ford, *The Attentive Life: Discerning God's Presence in All Things* (Downers Grove, IL: InterVarsity Press, 2008), 67.

6. Nicholas G. Carr, *The Shallows: What the Internet Is Doing to our Brains* (New York: W.W. Norton and Co., 2011), 219.

7. Heather White, esq., "Connecting Today's Kids with Nature: A Policy Action Plan," *Be Out There: National Wildlife Federation*, May 2008, 1, http://www.nwf.org/~/media/PDFs/Campus-Ecology/Reports/CKN_full_optimized.ashx.

8. This term was coined by Richard Louv in *Last Child in the Woods: Saving Our Children from Nature-Deficit Disorder* (New York: Algonquin Books, 2008).

9. Richard Louv, *The Nature Principle: Reconnecting with Life in a Virtual Age* (New York: Algonquin Books, 2012).

10. Ben Klasky, "Connecting with Nature: There's an App for That," *Huffpost Green*, December 4, 2014, http://www.huffingtonpost.com/ben-klasky/connecting-with-nature-th_b_6266890.html.

11. Emily Schiola, "Top 5 Best Free Nature Apps for iPhone and Android," *Heavy*, September 1, 2015, Heavy.com, accessed January 26, 2016, http://heavy.com/tech/2015/09/top-5-best-free-nature-wildlife-outdoor-apps-for-iphone-android/.

12. Kathleen Norris, *The Quotidian Mysteries* (New York: Paulist, 1998), 70.

13. Frederick J. Gaiser, *Healing in the Bible: Theological Insight for Christian Ministry* (Grand Rapids, MI: Baker Academic, 2010), 170.

14. Ibid., 157.

15. Ibid.

16. Henri J. M. Nouwen, *Reaching Out: The Three Movements of the Spiritual Life* (New York: Image Books, 1986), 36.

17. William Placher, *Mark*, Belief: A Theological Commentary on the Bible (Louisville, KY: Westminster John Knox Press, 2010), 154.

18. Lamar Williamson, *Mark*, Interpretation Commentary Series, ed. James Luther Mays (Louisville, KY: Westminster John Knox, 2009), 198.

19. Gaiser, *Healing in the Bible*, 168.

20. Cathy Caruth, *Trauma: Explorations in Memory* (Baltimore, MD: Johns Hopkins University Press, 1995), vii.

21. Cf. Luke 17:19, see Gaiser, *Healing in the Bible*, 177.

22. Joanna Dewey, "Mark," *Feminist Biblical Interpretation: A Compendium of Critical Commentary on the Books of the Bible and Related Literature*, ed. Luise Schottroff and Marie-Theres Wacker (Grand Rapids, MI: Eerdmans, 2012), 31.

23. Gaiser, *Healing in the Bible*, 223.

24. Ibid., 249.

25. Ibid., 178.

26. Ibid., 237–38.

27. Ibid., 238.

28. Many studies exist about attendance at religious worship services, and much of it is contradictory. This article by Kelly Shattuck interrogates recent survey data to conclude that attendance is dropping, and fairly significantly. See "7 Startling Facts: An Up-Close Look at Church Attendance in America," ChurchLeaders.com, accessed January 27, 2016, http://www.churchleaders.com /pastors/pastor-articles/139575-7-startling-facts-an-up-close-look-at-church -attendance-in-america.html.

29. Alain de Botton, *Religion for Atheists: A Non-Believer's Guide to the Uses of Religion* (New York: Vintage, 2013), 83.

30. Sameer Rahim, "Alain de Botton Puts Faith in Temples for Atheists," *The Telegraph*, January 30, 2012, accessed January 27, 2016, http://www.telegraph .co.uk/culture/books/authorinterviews/9045391/Alain-de-Botton-puts-faith-in -temples-for-atheists.html.

31. It is worth mentioning that some fellow atheists have taken issue with de Botton's proposal that religions are distinctive in their encouragement to be other-focused. See James Croft's review of the book at "A Review of Alain de Botton's Religion for Atheists," *The Humanist*, May/June 2012, via Patheos, accessed May 23, 2016, http://www.patheos.com/blogs/friendlyatheist/2012/04/21/a -review-of-alain-de-bottons-religion-for-atheists/.

32. Diana Eck, *Encountering God: A Spiritual Journey from Bozeman to Banaras* (Boston: Beacon Press, 1993), 153.

33. Ibid., 154.

34. See Fred Lehr, *Clergy Burnout: Recovering from the 70 Hour Work Week . . . And Other Self-Defeating Practices* (Minneapolis: Fortress Press, 2005); Jimmy

Dodd, *Survive or Thrive: 6 Relationships Every Pastor Needs* (Colorado Springs: David C. Cook, 2015); Anne Jackson, *Mad Church Disease: Overcoming the Burnout Epidemic* (Grand Rapids, MI: Zondervan, 2009), to name just a few.

35. Michael Frost, *Incarnate: The Body of Christ in an Age of Disengagement* (Downers Grove, IL: InterVarsity Press, 2014), 208.

36. Cheryl M. Peterson, *Who Is The Church? An Ecclesiology for the Twenty-First Century* (Minneapolis: Fortress Press, 2013), 126.

37. Wayne Muller, *Sabbath: Finding Rest, Renewal, and Delight in Our Busy Lives* (New York: Bantam Books, 1999), 89–90.

38. Simone Weil, *Waiting for God* (New York: G.P. Putnam and Sons, 1951), 227, as quoted in Ford, *The Attentive Life*, 49.

39. Frost, *Incarnate*, 168.

40. See my discussion of Luther's approach to scripture as law and gospel in *Crossing the Divide*, 114–15.

41. Johann Baptist Metz, *Faith in History and Society: Toward a Practical Fundamental Theology*, trans. David Smith (New York: Seabury Press, 1980), 185, quoted in Shannon Craigo-Snell, *The Empty Church: Theater, Theology, and Bodily Hope* (Oxford: Oxford University Press, 2014), 108.

42. Serene Jones, *Feminist Theory and Christian Theology: Cartographies of Grace* (Minneapolis: Fortress Press, 2000), 172.

43. Peterson, *Who Is The Church?*, 134.

44. Daniel Migliore, *Faith Seeking Understanding: An Introduction to Christian Theology*, 2nd ed. (Grand Rapids, MI: Eerdmans Publishing Company, 2004), 244.

45. "Should Our Worship Go Digital?" Ken Chitwood, *Lutheran Church Extension Fund Leader to Leader Blog*, March 23, 2015, http://blog.lcef .org/2015/03/23/should-our-worship-go-digital/.

46. Bob Hyatt as quoted in Anne Hammock, "Online Churches Draw Believers, Critics," *CNN*, November 15, 2009, accessed February 3, 2016, http:// www.cnn.com/2009/TECH/11/13/online.church.services/index.html?eref=ib _us.

47. See Bob Hyatt, "Virtual Church Is STILL a Bad Idea," *Christianity Today Blog*, October 27, 2009, http://www.christianitytoday.com/le/2009/october-online-only/virtual-church-is-still-bad-idea.html.

48. Hammock, "Online Churches Draw Believers, Critics."

49. Ibid.

50. "Extravagence United Church of Christ," http://www.extravaganceucc.org/.

51. Jo Hudson, quoted by Carol Howard Merritt, "Virtual Real Presence," *Christian Century* (May 28, 2014), 43.

5. Beyond Digital Strategies

1. Guillermo Hansen, "The Networking of Differences That Makes a Difference: Theology and Unity of the Church," *Dialog: A Journal of Theology* 51, no. 1 (Spring 2012): 41.

2. Elizabeth Drescher, *Tweet If You Heart Jesus: Practicing Church in the Digital Reformation* (Harrisburg, PA: Morehouse Publishing, 2011) 85.

3. Ibid., 84.

4. David T. Bourgeois, *Ministry in the Digital Age: Strategies and Best Practices for a Post-Website World* (Downers Grove, IL: IVP Press, 2013), 51.

5. Meredith Gould, *The Social Media Gospel: Sharing the Good News in New Ways* (Collegeville, MN: Liturgical Press, 2013), 28–9.

6. Michael Frost, *Incarnate: The Body of Christ in an Age of Disengagement* (Downers Grove, IL: InterVarsity Press, 2014), 210.

7. See Pastor Wegner's discussion of how Granger's virtual connections are enhancing their ministry with and to one another, "Granger Community Church Launches the Table," accessed January 29, 2016, https://vimeo.com/31207862.

8. See "Social Media—The Table Project," accessed January 29, 2016. http://www.fellowshipone.com/customers/social-media-the-table-project.

9. Drescher, *Tweet If You Heart Jesus*, 110.

10. Ibid., 109.

11. Ibid., 111.

12. Ibid., 115.

13. Sophie Lebel and Gerald Devins, "Stigma in Cancer Patients Whose Behavior May have Contributed to the Disease," *Future Oncology* 4, no 5 (October 2008): 717–33.

14. Monica A. Coleman, *Not Alone: Reflections on Faith and Depression, A 40-Day Devotional* (Culver City, CA: Inner Prizes, Inc., 2012), 67.

15. Ibid., 67.

16. "How Do People Who Are Blind Use Computers and Other Technology?" *Wonderopolis*, accessed March 2, 2016, http://wonderopolis.org/wonder /how-do-people-who-are-blind-use-computers-and-other-technology/.

17. Julian Dailly, "Blind Young People Aren't Well Connected to the Internet . . . Yet," *The Guardian*, October 2, 2012, http://www.theguardian.com/media -network/media-network-blog/2012/oct/02/blind-digital-technology-internet -design.

18. As cited in Anne Hughes, Maria Gudmundsdottir, and Betty Davies, "Everyday Struggling to Survive: Experiences of the Urban Poor Living with Advanced Cancer," *Oncology Nursing Forum* 34, no. 6 (2007): 1113–18.

19. Ibid., 1118.

20. Emilie M. Townes, "'The Doctor Ain't Taking No Sticks': Race and Medicine in the African American Community," *Embracing the Spirit: Womanist Perspectives on Hope, Salvation and Transformation* (Maryknoll, NY: Orbis Books, 1997), 183.

21. Ibid., 191.

22. GFCA Legal Department, "HIPAA Privacy Rule and Local Churches," (Nashville: United Methodist General Council on Finance and Administration 2004), http://www.churchadminpro.com/Articles/HIPAA/HIPAA%20-%20 Privacy%20Rule%20and%20Churches.pdf.

23. See my posts "Top Ten Reasons for Using CaringBridge When Something Bad Happens," *Grace Blog*, September 1, 2012, http://hopingformoreblog

.blogspot.com/2012/09/the-top-ten-reasons-to-use-caringbridge.html, and "Top Five Challenges of Using CaringBridge When Something Bad Happens," *Grace Blog*, September 10, 2012, http://hopingformoreblog.blogspot.com/2012/09 /top-5-challenges-of-using-caringbridge.html, accessed March 2, 2016.

24. Daniel Migliore, *Faith Seeking Understanding: An Introduction to Christian Theology*, 2nd ed. (Grand Rapids, MI: Eerdmans Publishing Company, 2004), 268.

25. John Thatamanil, *The Immanent Divine: God, Creation, and the Human Predicament* (Minneapolis: Fortress Press, 2006), xi.